THE
Vampire
Watcher's
HANDBOOK

THE
Vampire
Watcher's
HANDBOOK
A guide for slayers

CONSTANTINE GREGORY

*Annotated by
Craig Glenday*

ST. MARTIN'S GRIFFIN
NEW YORK

For Jeannie and Jessica
"There is no cure for birth and death save to enjoy the interval"
GEORGE SANTAYANA

Text copyright © Craig Glenday 2003
Illustrations copyright © Chris Daunt/Illustration Ltd 2003
This edition copyright © Eddison Sadd Editions 2003

Library of Congress Cataloging-in-Publication Data available on request

ISBN 0-312-31504-X

First St Martin's Griffin edition: 2003

1 3 5 7 9 10 8 6 4 2

AN EDDISON•SADD EDITION
Edited, designed and produced by
Eddison Sadd Editions Limited
St Chad's House, 148 King's Cross Road
London WC1X 9DH

Phototypeset in Dutch 766 BT and Duc de Berry
using QuarkXPress on Apple Macintosh
Origination by Pixel Tech, Singapore
Printed and bound by Nordica International Printing Co., Hong Kong

Valid photo ID required for all returns, (except for credit card purchases) exchanges and to receive and redeem store credit. With a receipt, a full refund in the original form of payment will be issued for new and unread books and unopened music within 30 days from any Barnes & Noble store. For merchandise purchased with a check, a store credit will be issued within the first seven days. Without an original receipt, a store credit will be issued at the lowest selling price. With a receipt, returns of new and unread books and unopened music from bn.com can be made for store credit. Textbooks after 14 days or without a receipt are not returnable. Used books are not returnable.

Valid photo ID required for all returns, (except for credit card purchases) exchanges and to receive and redeem store credit. With a receipt, a full refund in the original form of payment will be issued for new and unread books and unopened music within 30 days from any Barnes & Noble store. For merchandise purchased with a check, a store credit will be issued within the first seven days. Without an original receipt, a store credit will be issued at the lowest selling price. With a receipt, returns of new and unread books and unopened music from bn.com can be made for store credit. Textbooks after 14 days or without a receipt are not returnable. Used books are not returnable.

Contents

✝

Are Vampires Real?

"The religion of one age is the literary entertainment of the next."

RALPH WALDO EMERSON

THE VAMPIRE – the fiendish, diabolical creature once feared above all others – has become a pale reflection of its former self. What once terrorized entire nations is now widely viewed as an effete, vaudeville villain, or even a fanged fancy-dress buffoon. It may still exert a certain power as a literary creation, but the truly monstrous being of previous centuries appears to have retired into the shadows.

But do not be fooled. The vampire is nothing if not durable. The bodies of animals and humans continue to be found drained of blood; witnesses still recount tales of attack by unseen, psychic entities; and a growing legion of occultists rank themselves among the undead, shunning light and banqueting on blood. It is time for the vampire hunter to once again dust off his stakes and prepare the holy water: we should not rest until these demonic aberrations have been eradicated for good.

Do not expect this book to be a historical or
sociological analysis of the vampire. It is not a
celebration of all things dark and gothic; and
neither is it a readers' companion to the vast
libraries of vampire fiction. You will care little
about Dr John Polidori's inspirations, Dracula's
subtext or the sociological significance of blood
when your own claret is being drained from
your body by the walking dead.

My intention is to arm the vampire hunter
not just with the necessary weapons to combat
the undead, but also an understanding of the
origins, habits, whereabouts and weaknesses of
this dastardly foe. I have drawn upon my own
experience, the treatises of priests and learned
men of science, and collated the salient points
into a practical guidebook for vampire watchers
and slayers alike.

The Vampire Watcher's Handbook comes
with one simple caveat: do not accept all you
read as the ultimate truth. If every vampire
account from history were taken at face value,
few would escape the vampire hunter's stake:
the infirm, the red-headed and the adulterous
are among the many suspected of this unholy
affliction over the centuries. Instead, use this
information to support your own judgement.
This book exists for those cases in which a
rational explanation cannot be found.

There are
sufficient mundane
explanations for
most cases of
vampirism – sleep
disorders, anaemia,
porphyria and
mania to name
just four – without
having to resort
to the paranormal

FOREWARNED IS FOREARMED.

CHAPTER 1

What are Vampires?

Believe for one moment that vampires are an anachronism, or the long-dead product of a bygone era, and you will sorely pay the price. The undead have always been – and still are – among us …

THE FEAR OF VAMPIRES – of half-dead creatures that attack us while we sleep; of forces that can drain us of our energy, will power or blood – is a primal instinct as ancient as our fear of darkness. Since the beginning of time, our dreams have been haunted by demons and spirits returned from the dead to seek revenge or sustenance. Or, perhaps, merely to terrify us.

For this is indeed the definition of the vampire as it is to be understood in this practical guide to their extermination. The creature may be a physical, tangible, flesh-and-blood being – a corpse possessed by an evil demon, perhaps – or reanimated as a result of black magic. It might even have no physical reality, existing somewhere between this world and the next as an incorporeal entity or wandering spirit.

Revenant = one who "comes back"

But irrespective of the form the vampire takes, two crucial traits unite and define these evil entities. The first – as the more pertinent label "revenant" implies – is the "undead" state of the creature: it is neither alive nor dead, but a corpse or soul which has returned from the grave to torment the living.

The second defining trait of a vampire is the requirement for sustenance, be it in the form of food, psychic or sexual energy, or blood. The vampire cannot maintain its undead state without feeding, and will stop at nothing to sate itself on flesh, blood or psyche.

This, then, is the immortal creature that stalked our ancestors and continues to stalk us today. Throughout this chapter I would like to touch on the origins and evolution of such creatures, in the hope of arming the vampire watcher and slayer with a full understanding of the great task ahead.

FIGURE 1

WOOD ENGRAVING, BRAM STOKER'S *Dracula* (1897). LUCY WESTENRA SUCCUMBS TO THE VAMPIRIC COUNT. IT IS FROM STOKER'S NOVEL THAT THE IMAGE OF THE SEDUCTIVE, ARISTOCRATIC VAMPIRE HAILS.

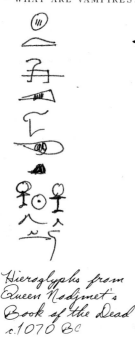

Hieroglyphs from
Queen Nodjmet's
Book of the Dead
c.1070 BC

As did the
Andean
cultures of
South America

† The Origins of the Vampire

THE BELIEF in the survival of the soul or spirit beyond physical death has been a fundamental aspect of humanity for at least the last hundred thousand years. This is evinced, I believe, by the treatment afforded to the dead since prehistory. Even the seemingly simple act of burying or cremating the dead is ritualistic. It is no mean feat to dig a pit large enough to accept a body; and burning a fully grown adult to anything resembling ash involves significant resources of effort and material. It is far easier simply to leave a body to decompose.

But if this is not enough to convince the reader that the soul's journey into the afterlife has always been of paramount importance, then consider the many and diverse rites that accompany death.

Our Neanderthal ancestors went to the trouble of burying their dead, but also ensured that the bodies were tied with the knees against the chest. Was this to mirror the foetal position and thus herald reincarnation? Or was it to prevent the physical body from reanimating after death?

Nowhere was the preparation and care of the dead taken more seriously than in Ancient

Egypt. Inscriptions dating back four thousand years, found on pyramid walls at Sakkara, detail the spells and rituals necessary to transport the dead to the "other side". It was believed that the health of the departed soul depended on the well-being of the physical body. This led to the introduction of mummification to help protect the body from dissolution. Riches, food and furniture commensurate with the regal status of the Pharaoh were buried alongside the body, as was the *Pert em Hru* ("Book of Coming Forth by Day") – a guidebook to aid the soul's passage into the afterlife. Failure to abide by these rules was believed to have terrible consequences for both the deceased and their surviving families: namely, vampirism, or the return of the body from the dead.

Pert em Hru is better known as the Book of the Dead

FIGURE 2

RAMSES II, EGYPTIAN RULER 1290–1224 BC. PRESERVATION OF THE DEAD ENSURED THE INTEGRITY OF THE PHYSICAL BEING; IF ILL-TREATED, THE DEAD MAY RETURN, VAMPIRE-LIKE, SEEKING SUSTENANCE.

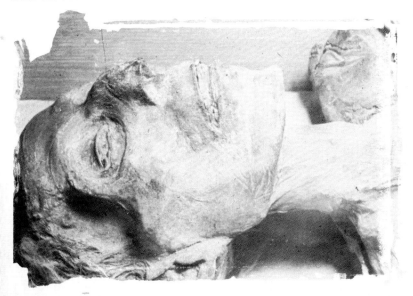

✝ The First Vampires

FIGURE 3
BABYLON CYLINDER SEAL
C.2000 BC. A FEMALE
VAMPIRE SITS ASTRIDE HER
SLEEPING MALE VICTIM,
WHILE A SECOND MAN
BEARS DOWN UPON HER
WITH A WEAPON.

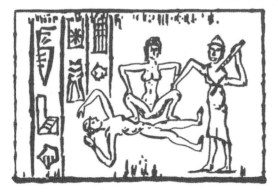

THERE CAN BE NO DOUBT that the vampire was known to our earliest ancestors. An engraving on a prehistoric drinking bowl, reproduced in the respected journal *Délégation en Perse*, depicts a man copulating with what is arguably one of the undead. The head of the revenant has just been severed, and it is believed that the image was intended as a warning to vampires to keep their distance or else face the inevitable consequence.

The earliest writings on vampiric entities can be traced back to the Babylonian and Assyrian states that rose in the Second Millennium BC. Here existed a hierarchy of spirits – ghosts, half-demons and demons – including vampire-like creatures that would return from their graves and torment the living. Among these were the "wind-like" *utukku*, an invisible or incorporeal demon; and, most significantly, the *ekimmu*, the soul of a departed person that was able to find no rest in death. Both of these tortured spectres were the result of death taking place under specific conditions – perhaps violently, prematurely or with certain tasks undone – or not having received appropriate burial rites. Unable to proceed into the Underworld, these spirits would return to earth, preying on the living for sustenance: "A hungry man is an angry man", as the old aphorism states.

The Babylonians also provided us with an early depiction of a vampire, one remarkably similar to that shown on the prehistoric bowl. Engraved on a cylinder seal is the image of a female vampire mounting a sleeping man. Over them stands another man wielding a sword or stake – again, a warning that any malignant entity should stay away or face execution. Cylinder seals were used to impress a unique, personalized "signature" into soft clay writing tablets. Like signet rings, they identified the status in society of the signatory, so we can safely assume that the owner of this seal was particularly fearful of vampiric attack.

"The gods which seize upon man
Have come forth from the grave;
The evil wind-gusts
Have come forth from the grave;
To demand the payment of rites and the pouring out of libations,
They have come forth from the grave;
All that is evil in their hosts, like a whirlwind Hath come forth from their graves."

Babylonian tablet inscription

Those considered potential vampires in Babylon:

- Women who die a virgin
- Women who die while breastfeeding
- Unmarried men
- Evil men
- Anyone buried in a shallow grave
- Anyone not given a burial at all
- Prostitutes

Powerful, life-
affirming charms:

ankh = "key of life"

Eye of Horus

Khat
means
"corruptible"

† Vampires in Ancient Egypt

*L*IKE THE BABYLONIANS and Assyrians, the ancient Egyptians possessed a haunting fear that their soul or spirit might suffer in – or not even reach – the afterlife if the physical body was not shown due reverence. And that a wandering soul finding no rest or sustenance in Heaven was apt to return to haunt the living. Thus it is the believed that true vampirism originated in the Nile Delta.

The Egyptians believed that every man and woman was composed of many different souls or states of consciousness: the exact number – and their definitions – is impossible for us to ascertain, but there may have been as many as nine different aspects of humanity, each one as distinct to the people of Ancient Egypt as are our senses to us today.

The *khat* was the physical manifestation of life. This was the body that would decay in the period following death unless it had first been properly mummified. Another element was the *ba*. Represented pictorially by a human-headed heron, hawk or falcon, the ba was that part of the soul capable of astral travel, taking flight from – and travelling independently of – the physical body.

✝

To those with a fascination for vampirism, the *ka* is the most intriguing aspect of Egyptian consciousness. This "double" was believed to be capable of wandering independent of the body. True immortality could be achieved only when the ka and the ba were united in the afterlife. For this to be possible, the ka required not only an uncorrupted body – hence the complex embalming rituals of Ancient Egypt – but constant oblations in the form of flowers, herbs, food and drink. A chamber dedicated to the ka would be built into tombs, and a full-time priest would ensure that offerings were made each day.

If the ka was not sufficiently provided for, it was feared that it would leave the tomb as a *kama-rupa* in search of its own sustenance – faeces, urine, brackish water and decaying animal. It was also believed that the ka, clad in its burial clothes or wandering naked, could attack the living, draining them of psychic energy or blood. No one was safe from this most ancient form of vampire.

When Egypt fell to the Persians in around 550 BC, this insistence on the preservation of the physical body faded. With the rise of Christianity, a reversal in the treatment of the dead meant that only the complete dissolution of the corpse could result in eternal life. The vampire would clearly have to adapt.

Other embalmers of the ancient world:

- *Aleuts – Aleutian Islands*
- *Guanches – Canary Islands*
- *Quechuas – Peru*
- *Chuchoros – Chile*
- *Anasazi – North America*
- *Dani – Papua New Guinea*

Could this have been the inspiration for the old "Mummy" horror movies?

15

✝ Vampires in the Middle Ages

*T*HE TURN OF THE FIRST MILLENNIUM saw the rise of reported vampire activity throughout the known world. This was an era that came to be known throughout feudal Europe as the "Age of the Antichrist". Indeed, Michel de Notredame, in a famous epistle to King Henry II, warned of the coming of the "Empire of the Antichrist", and even Popes were denounced as agents of the Dark Lord himself.

If accounts from the medieval chroniclers are to be believed, perhaps the Antichrist was indeed stalking the land, reanimating corpses for His own wicked means. William of Newburgh, the author of the twelfth-century *Historia Rerum Anglicarum* ("History of English Affairs"), talks of "certain prodigies" in his work:

> *"It would not be easy to believe that the corpses of the dead should sally (I know not by what agency) from their graves, and should wander about to the terror or destruction of the living … did not frequent examples … suffice to establish this fact, to the truth of which there is abundant testimony."*

Newburgh recounted the tale – among many others – of a chaplain "with little respect for his sacred order". Upon his death, the apostate cleric returned from his grave to terrorize his mistress who, in turn, enlisted the protective services of two priests. The revenant was tracked to his grave, attacked with an axe (which had little effect on the ruddy chaplain, despite cleaving enormous holes in his torso), and then finally burned to ashes.

Over the centuries that followed, countless similar cases would be reported the length and breadth of Europe. Confined almost exclusively to the peasant classes, these accounts were so remarkable in their similarity that only one logical conclusion could be drawn – that *cadaver sanguisugus* was among us. We can only speculate that had these terrifying "blood-sucking corpses" spent more time pestering the elite classes then greater efforts might have been made to curb their ferocious advance throughout medieval Europe.

THE NOBLE SAVAGE

A fifteenth-century nobleman and compatriot of Joan of Arc, Gilles de Rais indulged in savage and sadistic acts of sexual cruelty and cannibalism, earning him a reputation as a bloodthirsty vampire. A patron of the black arts, de Rais was believed to have "invoked and conjured evil spirits" to help him kill as many as eight hundred people, most of them children. He was finally captured in 1440 and burned at the stake.

While not a genuine revenant, he was one of the first in a long line of nobility to be branded a vampire, and perhaps the origin of the enduring idea that vampires are charming and aristocratic.

† Vampires and the Reformation

Signature from a 17th-century letter – purports to be that of a demon who made a pact with the priest Urban Grandier

UNTIL THE REFORMATION – the overhaul of the Catholic Church during the fifteenth century – accounts of vampirism had been marginalized to anecdotes noted in chronicles. This changed with the papal sanctioning of a number of publications describing vampires and techniques for their prevention. Thus, the vampire now had the official recognition of what ought to have been its natural enemy.

The first treatise to deal seriously with the occult was *Malleus Maleficarum* ("Witch Hammer"), published in 1485. The pretext for this handbook – intended as a practical guide to hunting and eliminating witches and demons – came from the Bible (Exodus 22, *18*): "Thou shalt not permit a sorceress to live." Its Dominican authors, Johann Springer and Heinrich Kraemer, offered dubious advice for dealing with witches and vampires, both of which were considered patent manifestations of the Devil. Thus was born a period of hysteria that saw the torture, drowning, hanging and burning of countless innocents across Europe – an era that would last for several centuries.

More significant works followed. Scotland's King James VI (James I of England) gave the

vampire a royal seal of disapproval by collecting †
tales of the undead in his *Demonologie* (1597).

A significant thesis on vampirism during this period was *De Quorundum Graecorum Opinationibus* (1645), a cornucopia of Greek religious superstitions and ordinances collated by Father Leo Allatius.

Another respected figure at this time, the English philosopher-poet Henry More, wrote *An Antidote to Atheism* (1652) which, if little more than a collection of ghost stories, gave credence to what had previously been con-sidered simply a foul curse on the poor. Here was confirmation that the vampire was not just rising up through the ground, but also through the ranks of society.

"*Concerning Greek Superstitions*"

THE BLOODY COUNTESS

Erzsébet Bathory (1560–1614) may not have drunk the blood of her victims (although this cannot be ruled out), but she certainly did bathe in it.

Born into a powerful Hungarian family, Bathory earned her sanguinary *nom de plume* by torturing and bleeding dry young virgin girls. She believed that youthful blood had a restorative effect on her own ageing skin, and would regularly anoint – and even shower – herself with copious amounts.

Like Gilles de Rais before her, Bathory was not a vampire. She may have been an initiate of the black arts, and enjoyed bloody orgies, but it was only her lust for blood that secured *la comtesse hongroise sanguinaire* her place in the vampire pantheon.

† Vampire Epidemics

So called because it was thought that vampires would chew on their shrouds in the grave

THE GROWING CANON of vampire literature in the sixteenth and seventeenth centuries could have meant only one thing: Europe was in the grip of a major vampire epidemic. In his influential *Dissertatio Historica-Philosophica de Masticatione Mortuorum* ("Historical and Philosophical Dissertation on the Chewing Dead") (1679), German author Philip Rohr reiterated the belief that there was a satanic explanation for this evil curse: "The principal cause is the Devil himself ... he is indeed the craftiest of enemies, a foe who is ever seeking every occasion and opportunity to hurt and harm poor wretched mortals."

Thereafter, vampirism seemed to spread rampantly across Europe. Suspected corpses, exhumed at an alarming rate, were almost always found exhibiting the classic symptoms of vampirism: rubicund and replete bodies with tight drum-like skin, and mouths dripping with blood and still groaning from their half-digested sanguine feast. Pricked viciously with a stake they would cry out, their blood (or that of their victims) gushing forth in a fountain-like stream.

Of course, with little scientific knowledge of medicine or post-mortem decay, how else could our ancestors have accounted for their gruesome discoveries? Poor fellows stricken by mysterious poxes and suspected of being vampires were unceremoniously unearthed: showing the signs of their satanic affliction, their bodies were mutilated or staked. Of course, those wielding the stakes – and the horde of spectators that would invariably amass – also came into contact with the plague-ridden corpse and soon became infected themselves.

A deadly plague could spread easily under such ignorant circumstances, with the finger of blame placed squarely on the Devil and his vampiric minions. The more bodies that were exhumed, the more vampires were found; and the more vampires that were found, the more villages would be decimated.

PETER PLOGOJOWITZ

The following tale appeared in the much respected *Lettres Juives* ("Jewish Letters") (1729) by the Marquis d'Argens.

In 1725, a Serbian peasant farmer named Peter Plogojowitz died at the age of 62, only to emerge from his grave three days later. At midnight, he visited his son in search of food, and was duly offered a good plateful. He returned two nights later, at which time the son refused his request for more food. The next day, the son was found dead, and fellow villagers awoke complaining that Plogojowitz had tormented them in their dreams. Widespread lethargy and anaemia followed, and within a week nine had died. Plogojowitz was clearly a vampire and had to be destroyed.

The body was exhumed and found to be ruddy and plump. Blood oozed from the mouth, and his hair and nails had continued growing. A stake was hammered through his heart, soaking the grave in blood, and a funeral pyre was erected. Plogojowitz was reduced to ash, and his "victims" reburied with protective whitethorn and garlic. Thereafter, the nightly attacks ceased.

† Official Accounts

Y THE START of the eighteenth century, the vampire had infiltrated the upper reaches of society, from the universities and military academies to the churches and royal courts.

Increasing amounts of anecdotal evidence from across Europe seemed to support the existence of vampires. The same was even true in the New World, where the Spanish *conquistadors* returned from their travels with tales of the *civatateo* witch-vampires.

Accounts of the stirrings of reanimated corpses were gradually legitimized through their publication in countless dissertations and treatises by the world's most learned men. Among these

---

ARNOLD PAOLE

There are few cases of vampirism as well documented as that of Arnold Paole, a Serb who returned from the grave to terrorize the village of Meduegna, near Belgrade. The official police account, *Visum et Repertum* ("Seen and Discovered"), was published in 1731 by Dr Johann Flückinger, and countersigned by other respected eyewitnesses.

A soldier, Arnold Paole had returned from a tour of duty in the revenant-infested Greece. In 1728, he fell to his death, but not before sharing an account of a vampire visitation he had experienced in Greece.

Within a month of his death, Paole was seen wandering nightly through the village. Many complained of harassment from his reanimated corpse, some dying in mysterious circumstances. A suspected vampire, Paole was disinterred and found with "jaws gaped wide open ... lips moist with new blood". Garlic was scattered over the corpse and a stake plunged through the chest. The bodies of those thought to be Paole's victims were also exhumed and given similar reparation.

---

were tracts on the eating habits of the undead: ✝
De Masticatione Mortuorum in Tumulis ("On the
Masticating Dead in their Tombs")(1728) and
*Tractatus von dem Kauen und Schmatzen der
Todten in Grabern* ("Treatise on the Chewing
and Eating Dead in their Graves") (1734), both
by Michael Ranftius; and Christopher Rohl
and Johann Hertel's *Dissertatio de Hominibus
post Mortem Sanguisugis* ("Dissertation of the
Bloodsucking Dead") (1732).

Not wishing to be overshadowed by men
of science, the Church countered with its
own contribution, published in Paris in
1746: *Dissertations sur les Apparitions des
Anges, des Démons, et des Esprits; et sur les
Revenans et Vampires de Hongrie, de Bohême,
de Moravie, et de Silésie* ("Dissertation on
the Appearance of Angels, Demons, and
Spirits; and on the Revenants and Vampires of
Hungary, of Bohemia, of Moravia, and of
Silesia"). This significant work was created
by the Benedictine Dom Augustin Calmet.

The accompanying increase in literacy
during both the seventeenth and eighteenth
centuries contributed not only to spread of
vampirism – or at least of vampire tales – but
also, thankfully, to the dissemination of more
thoughtful, considered essays on the subject.
The Age of Enlightenment was fast approaching
and, as any worthy vampire slayer knows, light
can be particularly injurious to the undead.

Sample of the Devil's (alleged) handwriting. No one knows what it means – it's indecipherable.

† Vampires and the Enlightenment

*T*HE INTELLECTUAL REVOLUTION of the eighteenth century that became known as the Enlightenment saw the abandonment of many entrenched customs, heralding a new scientific age of reason. It was a time of great change, and the beginning of the end for many beliefs and superstitions – especially in all things ghostly and vampiric.

Faith in science over superstition – and religion – saw a gradual decrease in reports of vampire activity. The empiricists and natural philosophers of the Enlightenment castigated the folklorists and religious fanatics for their belief in the undead. Meanwhile, the Church, while continuing to believe in the Devil and the resurrection, now refused to endorse accounts of vampires and witches.

VAMPIRE KILLERS

The nineteenth century saw the popular return of the term "vampire" to describe sadistic, bloodthirsty murderers – who were very much alive. The German serial killer Fritz Haarmann, for example, came to be known widely as the "Hanover Vampire" for his cannibalistic preying on as many as fifty young homosexual men. And the so-called "Vampire of Düsseldorf", Peter Kurten, strangled, raped and slit the throats of his victims, craving their blood just as – in his own words – an alcoholic craves liquor. "You cannot understand me," Kurten stated before losing his head at the guillotine. "No one can understand me."

One of the most influential philosophers of the Enlightenment was Jean-Jacques Rousseau (1712–78). He summarized the progressive – if ambiguous – attitude to vampirism in a letter to Archbishop Christophe de Beaumont:

> *"If there is in this world a well-attested account, it is that of the vampires. Nothing is lacking: official reports, affidavits of well-known people, of surgeons, of priests, of magistrates; the judicial proof is almost complete. And with all that, who is there who believes in vampires?"*

But was the paucity of vampire accounts from this period a consequence of a greater understanding of the mechanics of death? Or was it the unwillingness of science to publish reports of activities consider too demonic, too pagan, too irrational for dissemination? For, just as happened during the Reformation, pockets of Europe remained untouched by the new schools of thought. The illiterate Gypsy populations that travelled to the remote parts of Hungary, Serbia, Romania, Russia and Greece continued to report encounters with the undead. And bodies continued to be unearthed, staked and cremated in the time-honoured fashion well into the nineteenth century.

But even if the vampire had been killed off by science, it was about to be resurrected by a new master: Romantic literature.

20th-century "vampires":

John Haig "Vampire of London" – drank the blood of his 9 victims and dissolved bodies in acid (1940s)

Andrei Chikatilo "Forest Strip Vampire" – cannibalized and vampirized at least 50 victims (1970s–1990s)

Juan Koltrun "Vampire of Podlaski" – vampirized two of his 7 rape victims (1982)

Marcello de Anrade – sodomized, killed and drank blood of 14 young boys hoping to regain his youthful looks (1991)

25

† Literary Vampires

IN THE LITERARY SENSE, the vampire attained immortality at the end of the eighteenth century. Although fictional revenants of various sorts began to appear during the 1740s, it was not until the publication of Johann Wolfgang von Goethe's ballad *Die Braut von Corinth* ("The Bride of Corinth") (1797) that the vampire became known to a large audience.

Goethe's vampire is a lovesick young maiden who dies when her parents refuse to allow her to marry her paramour. She returns from the grave to consummate her love – although not as a feculent, abhorrent corpse, but as the beauty she was in life. The poem concludes with the vampire burning on a funeral pyre.

Further Gothic romances followed, with each new incarnation of the vampire deviating further from the monster of legend. In Dr John Polidori's novella *The Vampyre; A Tale* (1819) we encounter the aloof, aristocratic Lord Ruthven, whose "dead grey eye" and "deadly hue" attract the attentions of many a society lady. James Malcolm Rymer's *Varney the Vampire* (1847) developed this aristocratic theme by introducing the cruel, sadistic Sir Francis Varney, a cad who continually preys on beautiful young women, in spite of having already been hanged, shot and staked.

*"From my grave to wander
I am forc'd,
Still to seek The Good's
long-sever'd link,
Still to love the bridegroom
I have lost,
And the life-blood of his
heart to drink;
When his race is run,
I must hasten on,
And the young must 'neath
my vengeance sink."*

Excerpt from The Bride of Corinth, *Johann Wolfgang von Goethe (1797)*

The theme of vampire sexuality was given a degree of credibility by Sheriden Le Fanu, whose *Carmilla* introduces us to the "languid – very languid" lesbian temptress Micalla Karnstein.

The vampire's eternal fate was finally sealed with the publication of Bram Stoker's seminal *Dracula* (1897). Drawing on the rich characters and gothic horror of earlier vampire fiction – and expertly weaving in Eastern European folklore, such as the legend of Vlad Tepes, "The Impaler" – Stoker created an unforgettable monster that will haunt the world forever.

However, as far as "real" vampires are concerned, Dracula proved to be the final nail in the coffin. For the bloodsucking beasts of folklore have now been usurped by a fictional creation whose power over us is greater than that of any revenant. But has the fiend of folklore gone forever? Or could it merely be lurking in the shadows, biding its time?

FIGURE 4
COVER, *Dracula* (1897). BRAM STOKER CLAIMED THAT THE IDEA FOR HIS BLOODTHIRSTY ANTI-HERO FIRST APPEARED IN A NIGHTMARE BROUGHT ON BY AN EXCESS OF DRESSED CRAB.

DRACULA

6d.

BY

BRAM STOKER

6d.

WESTMINSTER
Archibald Constable & Co Ltd
2 WHITEHALL GARDENS

CHAPTER 2

Identifying the Undead

There can be no more unholy an act – no more cruel a fate – than the transformation of a soul into a vampire. But like most afflictions, preventative action can be taken if the symptoms are diagnosed early enough.

HAT IS A VAMPIRE? Accounts and descriptions of the vampire vary perhaps more than any other creature of folklore, mythology or legend. Even the most popular defining attributes – the lust for blood, photosensitivity, fear of garlic and religious symbols – fail to cross international boundaries with any consistency. All of which makes it impossible to give a single satisfactory description of the beast's origins, physical appearance, habits and motivations. Similarly, neither can the causes of this unholy affliction be diagnosed satisfactorily. What is considered a curse in one part of the world is to others a gift, a power bestowed upon only the most fortunate.

All that can be stated with any certainty is that if you are unfortunate enough to encounter one of their ranks, he is unlikely to be a nobleman

with a widow's peak and a penchant for black. †
Indeed, you are more likely to come face to ugly
face with a fetid, shambling corpse with rotting
grave clothes and equally putrid breath.

I hope to paint a general picture of the
many different species of creature that the
international vampire hunter may encounter. I
will also attempt to map the various roots of
this evil, in the hope that some unfortunate
souls may be saved from their eternal fate.

First, let me reinforce the caveat issued in
the introduction: throughout this humble
manual I describe crea-
tures that may be
merely the figment of
paranoid, superstitious
and uneducated minds.
I cannot vouch for the
reality of every form
of revenant described
herein; I have simply
collated my personal
findings with those of
other investigators in
the hope that the
hunter is sufficiently
armed. It may not be
possible to predict the
terrors that await, but
you can at least prepare
for them.

FIGURE 5

EARLY TWENTIETH-CENTURY
AUSTRIAN LITHOGRAPH
DEPICTING THE VAMPIRE
AND HIS BLEEDING FEMALE
VICTIM. ONE OF MANY
POPULAR PORTRAYALS NOT
SUPPORTED BY FOLKLORIC
REPORTS OF SHAMBLING,
REVITALIZED CORPSES.

† Congenital Vampirism

*T*HERE ARE SOME who are unfortunate enough to be born under the curse of the vampire. These are the ill-fated souls for whom undeath is inevitable. They may pass through this life unaware of the diabolical future that awaits them; or they may be forced to live in constant fear of the stake and pyre. These poor creatures have little choice about death: they will almost certainly return as a vampire.

BORN WITH A CAUL: The caul is a thin membrane that surrounds the foetus in the womb. Some babies are born with a sheet of "film" clinging to their heads. In some parts of the world, this is considered lucky, able to grant the child a sixth sense or protect it from drowning.

To others, a caul – in particular, a dark red caul – indicates that, upon its death, the child will return as a vampire. The only recourse is to desiccate or burn the caul and sprinkle it into the child's food. Otherwise, when this person dies, the body must be treated as a vampire.

OFFSPRING OF A WITCH: Anyone who practises black magic, witchcraft or Satanism is playing with their children's lives. The offspring of women hanged, drowned or burned as witches were considered likely to return as vampires.

Or those born with:

- a tail
- unusually thick hair
- all-over body hair
- joined eyebrows
- red cheeks
- a cleft palate
- blue eyes

OFFSPRING OF THE DEVIL: Catching the Devil's eye may be enough to turn a foetus into a vampire. Mothers who know Satan carnally are guaranteed to give birth to a vampire, if not the Antichrist himself. "Children this begotten by Incubi are tall, very hardy and bloodily bold," we are told in Reverend Father Ludovico Maria Sinistrari's *De Demonialitate*, and also "arrogant beyond words, and desperately wicked".

ILLEGITIMACY: The nosferatu is the illegitimate child of illegitimate parents. "The living vampire is in general the illegitimate offspring of two illegitimate persons," wrote Mme. Emily de Laszowska Gerard, author of *Transylvanian Superstitions*, "but even a flawless pedigree will not ensure anyone against the intrusion of a vampire in his family vault, since every person killed by a nosferatu becomes likewise a vampire after death".

SEVENTH SON: Being born the seventh son of a seventh son is a blessing to some, a curse to others. To the Irish, this bestows the child the powers of healing and "second sight"; to the Romanians, it is a guarantee of vampirism.

BORN ON A RELIGIOUS DAY: In some Slavonic countries, and also particularly Greece, it is considered to be a curse – and a sure sign of vampirism – if you are born on a holy day.

Also considered undead:

- *He whose mother dies in childbirth*
- *Children of prostitutes*
- *Those born with extra nipples*
- *Extensively birthmarked*

(Take these all with a pinch of salt)

The callicantzari are a particularly heinous species of vampire born between Christmas Day and Epiphany

31

† *Accidental Vampirism*

ANY ONE OF US can become a vampire if the decisions we make in life take us down the wrong path. If mythology and folk tales are to be believed, the risk is very great.

VAMPIRE ENCOUNTERS: As recounted in many works of literature, the bite or kiss of the vampire is enough to render any person one of the undead. Whether this happens immediately or later, upon your death, depends on the species of vampire to which you have fallen prey. Like the vampire bat, your attacker may return night after night, draining you slowly; or he might kill you outright, at which point you instantly become a bloodthirsty revenant.

BLACK MAGIC: Those practising the black arts are sure to rise from the grave.

LIVING A WICKED LIFE: Anyone who is evil, violent or murderous risks the curse of the vampire. Prostitutes, liars, thieves, adulterers, apostates and, indeed, any other wicked person should expect to have their body treated as a vampire upon their death. In some cases (where vampirism results from excommunication) absolution may be sought, but otherwise a wicked life means certain undeath.

The German nachzehrer vampire can also kill with its shadow, which you must not let fall over you (or over a corpse)

AVENGING A MURDER: The only murderers who do not risk vampirism are those who kill to avenge another murder. In Greece, if a killer remains unpunished, the family of his victim may be struck down with vampirism – or at least haunted by the returned spirit of the deceased. If the murderer cannot be sought, a close relative, friend or spouse may suffice.

Where does this all end? Could set off a terrible chain reaction of murders!

LOVE WITHOUT HAPPINESS: According to Assyrian mythology, those who experience love but not happiness may continue living after death. The unmarried also run the risk of vampirism.

Especially those who die virgins

FIGURE 6
WOOD ENGRAVING,
HARTMAN SCHEDEL'S *Liber Chronicarum* (1493). THE WEREWOLF SYMBOLIZES MAN'S AGGRESSIVE, ANIMAL INSTINCT, AND IS CLOSELY RELATED TO THE VAMPIRE.

WEREWOLFISM: Lycanthropy – the state of being a werewolf – also carries a risk of vampirism after death. There are a number of supposed causes of lycanthropy: a bite from a wolf or werewolf; drinking water from a wolf's paw print; eating a sheep killed by a wolf; being born with a thick covering of body hair.

CURSE: Anyone who dies while under a curse can rise from their grave as a revenant. Of particular severity are curses placed on children by their parents.

✝ Causes of Vampirism at Death

OVER THE LAST THREE hundred years, the Church has defined vampirism not as reincarnation performed by the Devil – for reincarnation is the remit of God alone – but as the reanimation of a corpse by a passing demon. The mechanism by which the corpse becomes an empty receptacle for a mischievous entity may be triggered by any number of incidents.

SUDDEN OR VIOLENT DEATH: Any death that "shocks" the soul out of the body may leave the corpse susceptible to possession. Drowning, fatal accidents, murder and heart attacks are all prime examples.

IMPROPER BURIAL: A proper burial is paramount if vampirism is to be avoided. Any corpse left to rot in a shallow grave or ditch will find themselves not only prey to hungry feral animals but also to vampirism. This theory is based on the Christian requirement for the body to turn (or, in fact, *return*) to dust before the soul can properly enter Heaven. Without a proper covering of earth – the requisite six feet – it is believed that the body will not be able to properly decompose.

Related to this is the principle that a body must be buried in consecrated ground. Only under the spiritual protection of the church can the soul make its way successfully into the afterlife.

EXCOMMUNICATION: Those who have been excommunicated from the Church, or remain unbaptized or apostate, risk vampirism. A Greek sentence of excommunication runs: "Let him be separated from the Lord God Creator, and be accursed, and unpardoned, and undissolvable after death in this World, and in the other which is to come." For, without absolution, the body will "remain uncorrupted and entire in the grave ... possessed by some evil spirit, which actuates and preserves them from corruption ... and that they feed in the night, walk, digest, and are nourished, and have found ruddy in complexion."

PREMATURE BURIAL: Anyone mistaken for dead and given too hasty a burial risks having the soul shocked from their body. Some may be fortunate enough to wake from their catalepsy in time: consider the case of Cardinal Diego de Espinosa, Philip II's Grand Inquisitor, who awoke during his own embalming.

Not so fortunate are those cases who awake during their cremation – in *Historia Naturalis (VII)*, Pliny recounts the tale of Aviola, who

Note: Scratches on the inside of coffin lids could be the result of the cadaver's natural post-mortem movements

35

✝ awoke on his own funeral pyre but who could not be saved from the flames in time.

Even more appalling are those cases in which the "deceased" awakens after burial. Evidence for this most hideous of deaths comes from the many disinterred corpses found contorted into agonized positions. Such discoveries are evidence, to some, of vampirism, although before you push a stake through these unfortunate corpses consider the more likely explanation of premature burial.

FIGURE 7
PAINTING, *Inhumation Précipitée* (1854), ANTOINE-JOSEPH WIERTZ. INSPIRED BY EDGAR ALLAN POE, WIERTZ PLAYS ON OUR FEAR OF BEING BURIED ALIVE (TAPHEPHOBIA) – A NATURAL EXTENSION OF OUR FEAR OF DYING. COULD THIS EXPLAIN REPORTED CASES OF VAMPIRISM?

SUICIDE: In the eyes of God, taking one's own life is considered the ultimate presumptuous offence. This so-called "Act of Judas" is the

enemy of all things natural and life affirming, and thus a natural precursor to vampirism. In Ancient Greece, the hands of suicides were hacked off and reduced to ash: this, it was thought, would prevent the corpse attacking the living upon its inevitable return.

ANIMAL PASSING OVER THE CORPSE: An animal leaping or flying over a corpse or coffin may trap the departing soul on its way toward the afterlife. In such instances, the cadaver is left "empty" and becomes ripe for possession by an evil spirit. For this reason, in Scotland, pets are traditionally locked away until after a funeral; in England it is customary to kill any animal that comes into contact with the deceased. In a related ritual in Greece, it is considered an honour to protect the corpse of a relative or friend from animals; if an animal succeeds in overleaping the coffin, two sack needles are driven into the corpse, and the house decked out with thorny bouquets and showered with mustard seeds.

Not only animals prove a risk. In Russia, a corpse touched by winds blowing off the Steppes will reanimate, as will a Chinese cadaver struck by a beam of moonlight. Passing a candle over a coffin puts the incumbent at risk. And, should the shadow of a vampire fall on the corpse or coffin, expect to see the deceased walking among the living later that night.

† Describing the Vampire

THE NOTED STAGE PRODUCER and actor Hamilton Deane has a lot to answer for. He is the gentleman who introduced into our psyche the image of the pale, fanged and caped vampire. His stage portrayal of Bram Stoker's eponymous Count Dracula has spawned an immortal legion of undead minions, all dressed in elegant black evening attire. His was not the first stage depiction – that was in 1897 – but it was effectively the last.

Unlike a true vampire, Mr Deane's stage creation failed to account for the possibility that the corpse has festered in its grave for up to forty days. Its wrapping sheet, shroud or burial clothes would already smell of the putrescent skin beneath – the stench anything but romantic or captivating.

So, for those more accustomed to the charming vampire of fiction, here is a feature-by-feature profile of the undead creature of folklore and legend.

IN GENERAL: Expect the vampire to smell of putrefying flesh: an unmistakable odour, not unlike ammonia. Beware, however, that certain vampires – the Filipino *mandurugo*, the Irish *leanshaum-shee* and Malay *langsuir* – may radiate a stunning beauty that lures men to their death. Others have the ability to transform into beasts or even mists.

Now Malaysia

SKIN: Usually described as grey and pallid. The vampire's pale complexion may take on a ruddy glow after feeding on blood. In Greece, the term *tympaniaios* refers to the tight drum-like skin of a revenant that has just feasted on blood. Furthermore, the skin may be scaly or desquamate when burned.

Note: Don't stake a sufferer of anaemia (deficiency in red blood cells) or psoriasis (scaly, flaky skin) in the mistaken belief that he is a vampire!

HAIR: In Serbia and Romania, red hair is a sign of vampirism – an idea rooted in the belief that Judas Iscariot had red hair.

All-over body hair is rare, but not unknown: the Chinese *chiang-shi* has white or green hair all over its body. Malaya's beautiful *langsuir* has ankle-length black hair that hides a hole in the small of the back.

Bram Stoker's portrayal of vampires having hairy hands has no basis in folklore or legend, although some witnesses have described a downy fuzz covering the vampire's palms.

EYES: In years gone by, any corpse found in its grave with eyes wide open would be treated as a vampire. In Romania, a corpse found with one eye open and one closed is considered to be in the process of transforming into a vampire.

39

Don't go staking someone just because of their facial features!! We've moved on from the Dark Ages.

In Greece and the Balkans, blue eyes are a sign of vampirism; in other parts of Europe, the eyes of a vampire are red. To some witnesses, the eyes of a revenant are described as "hypnotic"; to others, they are black and lifeless, like those of a shark.

MOUTH: A cleft palate (harelip) – or any other facial disfigurement – may also be considered a feature of one who will return as a vampire. Even if not deformed, the lips and mouth may be bloodied from a feed, and pieces of flesh may still be trapped between the teeth. However, those close enough to smell its vile breath will find the stench to be the least of their concerns.

TONGUE: A barbed tongue identifies the owner as a Polish *upior* or Bulgarian *ubour*. In India, the *churel* has a jet-black tongue, while the Filipino *aswang* has a hollow tongue with which it sucks up the blood of its victims.

NOSE: The Bulgarian *ubour* has a single nostril. In general, the vampire's sense of smell is heightened and attuned to the bouquet of blood (but also very sensitive to perfumes, garlic, burning incense and faeces, all of which can be used to repel the bloodsucker).

Fingernails (and hair) appear longer post mortem owing to the retraction of the skin

FINGERNAILS: Long and talon-like. They may also be clotted with blood or mud.

TEETH: Infants born with teeth are considered by many to be potential vampires. (Note: not all vampires have fangs; the teeth of the African *asanbosam* are normal except that they are made of iron.) If the vampire bat is anything to go by, the teeth are razor sharp – so sharp that a bite may cause the victim no pain.

INTERNAL ORGANS: As strange as it may seem, vampires have internal organs – disinterred revenants have even been discovered eating their own organs.

The *penangalan* of Malaya is little more than a disembodied head that flies around with its intestines dragged behind.

In Europe, the heart and liver may be torn from a suspected vampire and burned to ash (like a witch, the liver of a vampire may be pure white). Note: the *strigoii* of Romania has two hearts.

THE STAGES OF DECOMPOSITION

Stage 1
- **Muscles relax**
- **Body cools (*algor mortis*)**
- ***Rigor mortis* sets in (for 1 to 2 days)**
- **Skin begins to shrink and retract**

Stage 2
- **Internal decay begins as bacteria and parasites become active**
- **If present, flies will lay eggs or deposit larvae in orifices**
- **Flesh begins to liquidize under the skin**
- **Skin slews off easily**
- **Maggots begin to migrate**
- **Gases cause the stomach to distend**
- **Dark bloody fluid discharges from orifices**
- **Trunk swells to almost twice original size**

Stage 3
- **Skin turns black and begins to break, deflating the corpse and releasing foul-smelling gases**
- **Decomposition continues until only the skeleton remains**

41

Vampire Traits
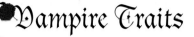

IF YOU ARE UNABLE to identify a revenant from its looks, you certainly will from its ungodly behaviour. Once again, put from your mind the nocturnal bloodsucker of fiction, for the many species of vampire have a wide range of habits that may surprise you.

MANDUCATION: Meaning simply "eating", this refers to the buried vampire's habit of chewing on its shroud or burial clothes. In his treatise *Masticatione Mortuorum in Tumulis Liber* ("The Eating Dead") (1728), Michael Ranftius lists numerous accounts from witnesses having heard pig-like snorting and snuffling sounds emerging from graves. Once disinterred, it was found that the corpses had devoured some or all of their cerements, and some had even begun eating their own flesh. In one sixteenth-century case, a man and a woman were found chewing on their own eviscerated intestines.

DIET: On the subject of eating, it is worth perusing the typical vampire's menu. As well as consuming their own flesh, the revenant will readily indulge in anthropophagy, the killing of a human being for cannibalism. A related habit is necrophagy, the eating of corpses that may be many days or even years old.

Another distasteful dish in the diet of the undead – particularly in India and Bulgaria – is animal or human faeces. This is perhaps why some vampires are recognized by their acute halitosis or stained teeth.

Finally, of course, the vampire's disgusting dinner is often washed down with a mouthful of blood. Do not expect the creature always to opt for the jugular: blood may be sucked from the chest or even the soles of the feet.

(Note: Vampires may also return to their family home for a favourite meal – followed by a demand for sexual intercourse.)

FLIGHT: A persistent misconception is that vampires can fly, or at least transmogrify into a winged beast. This is not true in all cases, but certain species have indeed mastered flight. The Filipino undead seem to have this ability, as do the Malay *langsuir*, the Chinese *chiang-shi* and some Serbian revenants.

DAYWALKING: D*aemonium merdianum* – the "noonday devil" – can walk the earth in daylight. Few vampires are purely nocturnal, so expect an evil encounter at any time of the day or night, especially if hunting in Eastern Europe.

HYDROPHOBIA: Water is the most natural of purifiers, so vampires are unable to swim or even cross running water.

In some parts of Europe the test for identifying revenants is the same as that once used for witches: the Iudicium aqua. The suspect is pitched into a river; if they float, they are demonic; if they drown, they are innocent.

43

† Psychic Vampires

PUBLISHED IN ENGLISH IN 1887, Adolphe d'Assier's *Posthumous Humanity* proposed that vampires did not even need to leave their graves to prey on the living; they could somehow detach and dispatch their astral body, which would seek out the living and drain their energy.

The idea of re-energizing the soul by psychically "sponging" off the living predates d'Assier's study by hundreds, if not thousands, of years. The ancient Assyrian *ekimmu* was a tormented spirit that returned to its family home to suck the lifeforce from relatives; the Bible tells of the ageing King David who, in order to revitalize himself, slept alongside a beautiful young virgin without "knowing her"; and in 1486 the Catholic Church recognized the existence of vampires by sanctioning the publication of *Malleus Maleficarum (see page 18)*, which discussed at length the existence of incubi and succubi, the psychic vampires that rape their victims as they sleep.

Incubi and succubi take their names from the Latin *incubare*, meaning "to lie on", as the first symptom of an attack by these diabolical creatures is a sense that something is sitting on the chest. It is generally accepted that the incubus is a male demon, and the succubus female (hence the ancient use of "succubus" to

Diabolical = dia, "two" + bolus "morsel" – i.e. mind and soul; an entity that preys on the mind as well as the body

mean "prostitute"), although in his eighteenth-century *Tractatus de Angelis*, Charles René Billuart argued that "the same evil spirit may serve as a succubus to a man and as an incubus to a woman".

Whatever the case may be, the effect is the same: the victim is left drained of energy. The nightly visitations may continue indefinitely – or until the prey has been psychically bled to death – and the victim may never know the cause of their infirmities.

But these are just two of the demons that indulge in nightly bouts of vampiric activity. In West Africa, the *obayifo* is a form of vampire that leaves it body to terrorize humans, cattle and even crops. This particularly menacing fiend has the ability to drink blood, even in its incorporeal form. The closely related *loogaroo*, found in the Caribbean, also leaves its body behind, travelling in search of blood in the form of a glowing orb of light. And the German *alp* is a shape-shifting demon that enters the dreams of its female victims via their mouth.

Even the living can have a vampiric effect on others. The Beberlang tribe of the Philippines claim to be able to astrally project from their bodies and vampirize their enemies. Initiates of the black arts can also train their minds to prey on weak individuals – in order to feed psychically or to increase their ranks with new "suggestible" members.

† *Symptoms of Psychic Attack*

NIGHTMARES: The very term "nightmare" refers to the *mara*, the nocturnal spirit that crushes its victims as they sleep, and vivid, terrifying nightmares are one possible sign that a psychic assault is taking place. Victims may have heightened sensory involvement, smelling, hearing and even feeling their attacker while being helpless to defend themselves.

CRUSHING FEELING: It can often feel as if a great weight is pressing down on the chest. This may be accompanied by an overwhelming sense of fear. In dreams, it may even be possible to see a creature perching on the chest or performing sexual intercourse.

LETHARGY: Following a psychic assault, the victim may feel lifeless, fatigued or emotionally drained. Those too frightened to sleep will themselves begin to look like walking corpses: gaunt, grey-skinned and drained.

"IMMACULATE" CONCEPTIONS: An incubus may leave more than a feeling of tiredness: some victims have reported pregnancies following an attack. Some are genuine, resulting in the birth of a child that – upon death – will return as a vampire. Others are phantom pregnancies: as *Malleus Maleficarum* explains, victims may be

Sounds like sleep paralysis –

- *sleeper feels paralysed*
- *crushing feeling*
- *frightened*
- *has visions*

Dhampirs are the offspring of a vampire and a mortal woman – see p.74

"seemingly pregnant, but on parturition, the swelling is relieved by an expulsion of a great quantity of wind".

UNEXPLAINED DEATH: There are many known cases of young, healthy people who simply die in their sleep from no known causes. In such cases, the psychic vampire is a likely suspect.

It should be noted here that not all cases of psychic vampirism happen at night – or, for that matter, intentionally. You may sometimes feel the presence of a psychic vampire during the course of the day, as your energy flags and your enthusiasm for everyday activity wanes.

Unintentional vampirism may also occur when those around you – quite possibly friends and relatives – drain you of emotion without being aware of the damaging effect they are having on you.

Investigate cases of SUNDs
(Sudden Unexplained Nocturnal Deaths)

- Normal, healthy people who die in their sleep
- No known cause of death
- Have other family members died similarly?
- What connects victims? Relatives? Proximity?
- Seek out a common person/relative who seems unaffected or full of energy; they may be the source of the problem

† Vampire Animals

I T IS A FACT OF THE NATURAL WORLD that vampire animals *do* exist. The common vampire bat (*Desmodus rotundus*) genuinely does suck the blood of the living, as does the vampire finch (*Geospiza nebulosa*), or sharp-billed ground finch, of Madagascar. It may not be a bloodsucker, but the hauntingly named *Vampyroteuthis infernalis* – quite literally, the "vampire squid from hell" – is a true creature of the deep, so named for its jet-black cape-like appearance and blood-red eyes.

However, these vampire animals need not concern the modern vampire slayer (although a more thorough study of *Desmodus rotundus* follows overleaf). Of greater importance are the animals under the direct control of the Devil. As we have seen, animals that leap over a recently dead body risk becoming possessed by the spirit of the deceased. Such accidental vampirism can be avoided by taking sensible precautions such as locking away pets between a death and the funeral.

Certain species of vampire are able to transmogrify into any animal at will, meaning that the vampire hunter must be suspicious of all types of animal he encounters during an investigation. The German *alp*, for instance, may appear in the guise of a dog, a pig, a bird

Snakes are particularly feared because of their connection with the serpent – i.e. Satan

or a snake; in the Balkans and parts of Asia, vampire butterflies and moths have been known to terrorize unwary travellers; and throughout Europe, dogs, wolves, owls and cats have all fallen under suspicion – indeed, during the witch hunts of the Middle Ages, cats were subject to trial by jury and even tortured and hanged for their association with witches.

Theriomorphic vampires – those that are able to change from human to animal form – are not easy to identify. One of the few signs of such a change is a wound inflicted on an animal that subsequently appears on a human. The vampires of Transylvania offer a pertinent example. Red-haired men who rise from the dead are believed to possess the power to transform themselves into frogs. Thus, any injury suffered by the frog would also appear on the corresponding body-part of the human.

Finally, be aware of animals that assist the vampire in its diabolical chores. In the Philippines, for example, be on your guard if, during the night, you hear a bloodcurdling "kiki kiki" birdsong – this is the sound made by birds that lead the bloodsucking *aswang* vampire to its prey. Similarly, the *chordewa*, the witch-vampire of Bengal, sends her malicious soul roaming in the body of an enslaved cat, and only the keen-eared will recognize the beast's peculiar mewling.

Vampire creatures:

Cats
Dogs
Snakes
Chickens
Turkeys
Pigs
Sheep
Birds
Flies
Butterflies
Bats
Frogs

49

† Vampire Bats

An anticoagulant called "Draculin" has just been isolated from the saliva of the vampire bat — doctors hope it might help combat heart attacks and strokes!

Don't get confused with other "false" vampire bats:

- Australian Giant False Vampire Bat (known as the "Ghost Bat" because of its grey/white colouring)
- African False Vampire Bat
- American False Vampire Bat

These are all carnivorous, but not blood drinkers

ONE OF THE MOST enduring images we associate with the vampire is that of the bat. Bram Stoker's *Dracula* is peppered with references to these supposedly menacing winged mammals: Lucy is pestered by a bat – the Count, presumably transmogrified – repeatedly buffeting against her window; Mina encounters Dracula in the form of a bat on her window-sill; Van Helsing describes to Harker "bats that come out at night and open the veins of cattle and horses and suck dry their veins".

Van Helsing is, of course, referring here to vampire bats. Of the 925 species of bat, there are three that do indeed drink blood. Although, given the fact they are restricted to Central and South America, the inhabitants of Transylvania have little to fear.

The common vampire bat (*Desmodus rotundus*) is a fascinating creature. For one, it is the only bat that is as nimble on the ground as it is graceful in the air. When it locates its prey, it lands nearby and, with a gait more akin to the crab, scuttles towards it silently. It then clambers over its body to find the most suitable spot for dining and, using its two canines, neatly trims away the fur. The skin is punctured by the two upper incisor "fangs". As the creature bites, it administers an anticoagulant that prevents the wound from clotting, allowing the bat to lap up the oozing blood with its specially adapted grooved tongue.

The vampire bat lives solely on blood – it is the only known mammal "singivore" – although it requires only a few tablespoons-worth each day. They choose to feed from slumbering cattle, horses, peccaries and birds, although have been known to drink the blood of snakes, lizards and crocodiles. I have even heard a first-hand account of a Mexican priest waking to find a still-bleeding vampire bite on the tip of his nose: vampire bats, he revealed, were at one time used in bloodletting ceremonies to heal the sick.

So forget the great, leather-winged terror of vampire fiction. No larger than your thumb, and with a wingspan measuring roughly eight inches, the only real risk vampire bats pose is the spreading of rabies, a disease which can decimate cattle populations. However, you should consider carrying a small bag of vampire bat bones with you when slaying: they will bring you luck – so say the Gypsy.

"Desmodus" = "bundled teeth". This refers to the closeness of the two central upper incisors.

FIGURE 8

ENGRAVING, *Le Vampire* (1838). THE VAMPIRE BAT HAS AN UNDESERVED REPUTATION AS A SERVANT OF EVIL – A MYTH PERPETUATED BY FANTASTICAL ACCOUNTS OF ATTACKS FROM GIANT SPECIES SUCH AS THESE.

A bat researcher died in Scotland this year from rabies

† Werewolves

FIGURE 9

THE WEREWOLF NEARS THE END OF HIS SUPERNATURAL TRANSFORMATION. DURING THE SIXTEENTH CENTURY, AN ESTIMATED THIRTY THOUSAND CASES OF LYCANTHROPY WERE REPORTED.

If possible, observe werewolf activity from the cover of a field of rye – the beast is repulsed by this type of crop

HERE IS MUCH cultural and religious heritage linking together vampires and werewolves. Both have the ability to alter their forms, both are driven by a lust for human blood and both claim their victims under cover of darkness.

Montenegrin legend has it that all vampires spend a gestational period as a werewolf, while Balkan mythology states that werewolves become vampires after their death. Indeed, it was commonly believed that anyone who died while under the curse of a werewolf would be reborn as a vampire.

Other beliefs from across the world attest to the link between these creatures of the night: in Serbia, the vampire and the werewolf are known by the same name – *vlkoslak*. And in China it was believed that – like werewolves – vampires were also covered in fur. The French fear the vampire-like *loublin*, a werewolf that digs up bodies in graveyards in order to feast on the flesh.

Tell-tale signs of lycanthropy – when the creature takes the human form – include broad hands with stubby fingers and hair in the hollow of the palm. It is common for the eyebrows to meet in the middle of the forehead, and the individual may take an unnatural pleasure in cruelty and extreme brutality. Beware of a man sleeping next to the casually discarded skin of a wolf. This may indicate a werewolf recently returned from its night of mayhem, exhausted by its excesses.

In its transmogrified state the werewolf is easier to recognize. Although able to turn into a terrifying and huge (in some cases the size of a calf) beast, a werewolf is unable to disguise the human intelligence in its eyes. As well as this sentience, the werewolf has superhuman strength that combines animal ferocity with human cunning. This is evident in the slaughter left in its trail. A werewolf will kill anything it comes across, spurred by its lust for blood and death. Scenes of carnage with mauled or half-eaten corpses – animal or human – is a good indicator of recent werewolf activity, especially if your find was preceded by a full moon.

Loup-garou = French for "shape changer"

53

† Zombies

*A*LTHOUGH ZOMBIES (or zombi) are not related to any vampire species, they may resemble the undead and share both their habits and habitat. The name is derived from the Congolese word *nzambi*, which refers to the spirit of a dead person, and in appearance they share the deathly pallor of a revenant. Unlike the vampire, however, they remain mute and oblivious to their surroundings, and are seemingly lacking any individual will.

This class of walking dead has its origins in black magic and the voodoo culture of Haiti. While vampires are the hideous result of Satanic or demonic intervention, zombies are "created" by a *bokor* – a voodoo sorcerer. These evil masters have the power to turn an innocent human victim into a compassionless killer. In recent times, the zombie has even acquired a reputation for vampire-like feeding on human flesh and brain matter.

Zombies are created by poisoning a victim with *poudre zombi*, a magical concoction that includes a toxin obtained from the puffer fish. This is potentially fatal to humans, so those that are not killed fall into a coma; the body becomes paralysed, heart activity falls to an imperceptible rate and the skin becomes cold and sallow. Believing that the person has died,

Scientists have identified the poison in puffer fish as a deadly nerve agent called Tetrodotoxin. It causes death in 50 per cent of people who ingest it.

preparations are made for burial. Some who have survived the experience have described being aware of their own funerals.

A number of days after burial, the *bokor* reverses the effects of the poison by using a cocktail of powerful drugs known as a "zombie cucumber". If the victim manages to survive, he or she will suffer extreme shock from the ordeal; brain damage and physical trauma are also likely side effects of the drugs. In such a condition, the zombie, unable to resist, is beaten and bullied into doing the will of the *bokor*. Historically, many have ended up as slaves on plantations.

Traditionally, zombies are destroyed either by burning or by decapitation.

There are many cultures in which people are more afraid of being turned into a zombie than of the creature itself. To prevent this, family members will sometimes stab the deceased through the heart or cut off the head. This is believed to free the soul from the reach of the *bokor*.

Check out George Romero's zombie movie trilogy:
- *Night of the Living Dead*
- *Dawn of the Dead*
- *Day of the Dead*

FIGURE 10

THE ZOMBIE RISES FROM HIS GRAVE. DESPITE THEIR SIMILARITY TO VAMPIRES, ZOMBIES ARE NOT DRIVEN BY UNCONTROLLABLE BLOOD LUST.

What if they're still alive?!

55

† Witches

FIGURE 11
THE WITCH COMMUNES
WITH NATURE. FOR
CENTURIES, THE CHURCH
CONSIDERED WITCHCRAFT
INDISTINGUISHABLE
FROM VAMPIRISM, AND
PUNISHED BOTH BY
TORTURE AND DEATH.

THE LINK BETWEEN WITCHES and vampires goes back hundreds of years. One of the earliest instances in print can be found in the pages of *Malleus Maleficarum* (1485). This treatise was concerned with the identification and destruction of European witches, and the fact that it was adopted by both the Catholic and Protestant church attests to its authority on the subject.

A Christian text, the *Malleus Maleficarum* classified all types of supernatural predator, be they witch or vampire, as the work of the Devil, thereby blurring the line between these different creatures. Regional, cultural and historical folklore has also created numerous variations in witch and vampire activities. Some believed that witches survived by eating the internal organs of their victims, while many others thought that vampires needed to imbibe human blood. Indeed, a creature regarded as a witch in one society may have been considered a vampire in another.

Distinguishing witchcraft from vampirism is relatively straightforward. Look for signs of repetitive and inexplicable bad luck or ill health in individuals or communities: all of this may indicate a witch's curse or hex. Also, sudden disappearances of pets in an area may suggest witchcraft, as small animals are commonly used in spells.

In rural areas where rumours of strange nocturnal gatherings or events abound, be on the lookout for signs of covens, forest clearings with evidence of fires, and the mysterious activities of a number of people. This may include a particular interest in herbology or pharmacology, an over-abundance of black cats or chickens, and an inclination to dance naked in the open air.

Remember that there is a difference between black magic and white (often Wiccan) magic. White witches can be an important ally in the struggle against vampires. Spells, potions and protective amulets offer defence from attack, and a prepared poultice – a cloth infused with herbs and other magical properties – can be placed over vampire bites to reverse its effects. An allied white witch may also be able to offer clairvoyant assistance or other forms of intuition to help you find and identify vampiric activity.

Witch-like vampire species:

- Africa – sbayifs
- India – chordewa, jigarkhwar
- Malaysia – bajang (male) & langsuir (female)
- Philippines – aswang (beautiful!!)
- Poland – brupsa (often takes on bird form)
- West Indies – loogaroo

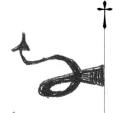

† Demons

IT WAS DURING the Middle Ages that the previously amorphous explanations for vampirism took on a solid shape: mischievous demons were taking possession of corpses and reanimating them for their own nefarious means.

This explanation would seem to make sense, since, in the Christian doctrine at least, demons were thought to be rebellious angels – led by Lucifer – whose aim was to carry out the evil wishes of their master on earth. But demons have been found throughout history and in nearly all major religions. Their specific characteristics and behaviour may differ according to local folklore but they are universally regarded as agents of destruction. Demons of a higher order can take a human form; lower orders manifest themselves in animals and – occasionally – objects.

FIGURE 12

THE DEMON RANKS ALONGSIDE THE VAMPIRE AS A MASTER OF EVIL. THE UNDEAD WERE ONCE THOUGHT TO BE UNDER THE CONTROL OF DEMONS INTENT ON WREAKING HAVOC.

Demons are ethereal, shapeless beings that exist beyond our sensory perception, but who must possess humans to perpetrate their foul business. This is done by entering a freshly dead body through the mouth, or by whispering hypnotic charms and seductions into the ear of their living victims. Once in control of a person – either dead or alive – the victim is forced to commit horrific acts of violence against friends and family, almost always ending in murder and suicide.

Identifying a body possessed by a demon goes beyond merely recognizing the physical aspects of a rejuvenated corpse. In human form, demons like to play games and often use charm and flattery to insinuate themselves into a person's company. They may be recognized by their preferred type of victim: attractive and vivacious individuals who mix in large and often influential circles.

Vampires and demons have shared a similar status in the doctrines of the Church of England since the Middle Ages. Both were actively hunted, and those suspected of demonic possession were decapitated or burned at the stake; corpses were often exhumed, examined and burned if evidence of demonic activity was found. In these modern times, exorcism is the more usual recourse for possession. Should you identify a case of demonic possession, share your observations and deductions with an allied priest whom you trust to find an acceptable solution.

Demons murder with ferocious energy – victims will show evidence of extreme brutality and blood loss

Signs of demonic possession:
- Insomnia
- Unbearable BO
- Severe fits and convulsions
- Coprolalia (Tourette-like outbursts of profanity)
- Xenolalia (speaking in other languages)
- Glossolalia (speaking in "tongues")
- Superhuman strength
- Appearance of inexplicable scars and wounds

CHAPTER 3

Finding Vampires

The domain of the vampire is no uncharted territory – others have gone before us and documented the habits of these reviled beasts.

FIGURE 13
THE VAMPIRE GORGES
HIMSELF ON A FEAST OF
BLOOD. THIS NEED FOR
SUSTENANCE UNITES ALL
SPECIES OF THE UNDEAD.

WITH THE VAMPIRE and his undead associates having been identified, we must next turn our attention to the potentially hazardous task of locating their whereabouts. In this chapter begins the practical instruction for the hunting of these ghoulish parasites. As before, the counselling that follows has been drawn widely from historical vampire lore across the globe.

The mythology, folklore and legend of almost every society are haunted by tales of the bloodsucking undead, from the *adze* of the Gold Coast to the *zmeu* of Wallachia. To aid the

Note: Gold Coast became Ghana in 1957

vampire hunter, some of the more rapacious
species are mapped out overleaf. However, it
must be remembered that the habits and
habitats of the vampire vary from country to
country – even region to region.

So, as the deerstalker familiarizes himself
with the territory, behaviour and tracks of his
quarry, so too must the vampire hunter
acquaint himself with the footprints of the
undead. To this end, I have listed the most
common signs of vampirism – both in an
individual and the community at large. Advice
is given on arming yourself sufficiently for the
hunt and, towards the end of the chapter, you
will find details of the numerous sites most
commonly associated with the undead.

Where to Look

The proactive vampire hunter should scour
newspapers and journals for clues that may
indicate the work of a vampire. Reports of
missing children, inexplicable crop blights,
cattle mutilations and rapid human or animal
depopulation could be discovered to have a
paranormal connection. Always be prepared to
remain open minded when you are faced with
such accounts.

Reports of organ theft also suggest vampiric
activity. The Indian *jigarkhwar* is just one of
the many vampiric creatures that crave the
taste of human organs.

† 𝔐apping the 𝔙ampire

IN ITS MANY FORMS, the vampire is a truly international blight. Those regions with a rich heritage of vampire lore are shown here, along with examples of the most common indigenous revenant species.

Africa: OBAYIFO
Tree-dwelling, child-eating vampire known to the Gold Coast Ashanti people.

Bosnia-Herzegovina: LAMPIR
Blood-drinking species destroyed only by fire.

Bulgaria: VAPIR, UBOUR
Rises after forty days in the grave to feed on blood, excrement and other "food".

China: CHIANG-SHI
White- or green-haired vampire with the power of flight and transfiguration.

Ireland: DEARG-DU
Rarely seen, sometimes appears in the form of a beautiful temptress.

Germany: NACHZEHRER
Shape-shifting vampire with psychic powers. Feasts on the bodies of the dead, and the blood – and energy – of the living.

Greece: VRYKOLAKAS
A night-walking creature that kills by crushing the chest of its sleeping victim.

ASIA

Pacific Ocean

AUSTRALASIA

Southern Ocean

N
W E
S

Nothing in Central / South America? Check out the Chupacabras ("goat sucker"), a blood-drinking vampire beast in Puerto Rico, Mexico and Brazil

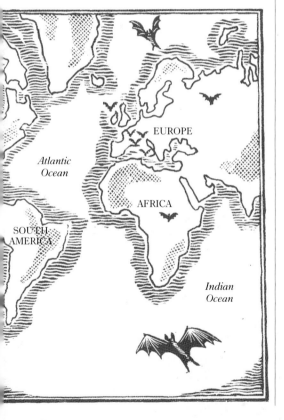

Malaya: LANGSUIR
Female vampire – usually of ravishing beauty – with long black hair concealing a blood-drinking organ in the back of the neck.

Philippines: ASWANG
Human by day, diabolical bloodsucker by night; prefers to feast on the blood of infants.

Romania: NOSFERATU
Bloodthirsty revenant that seeks sexual intercourse with the living.

STRIGOII, STRIGOII MORTI
"Living" and "dead" vampires which leave the grave to consume the living (both psychically and physically).

Russia: UPYR
Daywalking bloodsucker with a preference for children, which it eats with its iron teeth.

Slovenia: KUDLAK
Shape-shifting revenant associated with pestilence, plague and famine.

A lack of expected fauna may indicate a vampiric presence. A preternatural silence at dawn, an unexplained drop in the rodent population, reports of missing pets – all point to a predatory paranormal presence.

† Signs of Vampires in the Community

IT MAY BE POSSIBLE to detect the presence of a vampire by reading certain "signs" in the community. Dead bodies with fang-like bite marks, or graves opened from the inside, leave little room for doubt; others, such as those listed below, are more subtle manifestations.

FIGURE 14

THE BLOODLESS CARCASS OF A COW MUTILATED BY AN UNKNOWN ASSAILANT. SUCH DISTURBING FINDS ARE COMPELLING EVIDENCE OF VAMPIRIC ACTIVITY.

RESTLESS ANIMALS: Dogs are considered to be particularly sensitive to the undead, and may well react out of character when faced with a vampire. In parts of the Caribbean, anyone unduly harassed by a dog may be suspected as a servant of Satan. Horses, too, appear to be ill at ease when a vampire is close.

CATTLE DEATHS: The bodies of defenceless domesticated cows are often found horribly mutilated and, in some cases, completely exsanguinated – that is, without a single drop of blood left in them. To add to the mystery, the

↑ Looks like Chupacabra victims in Puerto Rico and Brazil. Is the goat-sucker a vampire?

surrounding area may be devoid of footprints or tracks, suggesting that the attacks have been carried out by some vicious winged beast.

One such suspect is the Bulgarian *ustrel*, a Saturday-born child that dies before baptism. Although not winged, this bloodthirsty spirit feasts almost exclusively on cattle, draining each animal before moving on to the next. Vampire bats can, of course, afflict cattle populations across Latin America, although never to such a devastating degree; and in Europe, where no such bat species exists, the cattle are equally at risk.

Other domesticated and <u>wild animals</u> have been found in similar states of mutilation: horses, sheep, goats, dogs, cats and even mice have fallen to this mystery attacker.

CROP BLIGHT: The undead are able to drain the lifeforce from any living thing, not only humans or animals. The Ashanti peoples of the African Gold Coast fear the *obayifo*, a revenant that prefers the blood of children, but is equally sustained by draining the energy from cacao crops. The pestilent *kudlak* of Slovenia also delights in the destruction of the harvest. In early Slavonic religions, the burial on holy ground of someone cursed or apostate was thought to result in the death of the local crops. It has even been suggested that the locust itself is under the control of the Devil.

Cattle mutilations are still common, although usually connected to UFO sightings. Vampire aliens, perhaps??

But vampire bats can *kill a herd by spreading rabies*

I've even seen photos of a whale and some seals mutilated in a similar way

Because blood = life, our ancestors would "water" their crops with blood

Vampiric conditions:

- *Haematomania – psychological obsession with blood*
- *Haematophilia – sexual arousal from seeing, drinking or smelling blood*
- *Haematodipsia – deviant need to see/drink/smell blood at any time (extreme form of haematophilia)*
- *Haematophagia – feeding on blood*
- *Renfield Syndrome – mental illness affecting emotionally unstable people (named after the insane fly-eating character in Bram Stoker's Dracula)*

✝ Signs of Vampires Among Individuals

THE INDIVIDUAL under physical or psychical attack from a vampire will present clearly identifiable symptoms. However, these may be very similar to those that result from more mundane conditions – conditions with which the vampire hunter must become acquainted.

As I explained earlier, many of the vampire "epidemics" of the eighteenth century were undoubtedly the result of medical ignorance and misunderstanding. Here follows a list of the common symptoms of vampirism.

BITE MARKS: The fang bite on the neck is largely a product of popular vampire literature. Instead, be on the lookout for non-healing wounds above the bridge of the nose, on the chest above the heart or between the breasts, on the wrists, or on the soles of the feet.

DEATHLY PALLOR: The victim of the vampire is readily recognized by his cold, pale appearance. Drained of blood, colour is lost in the cheeks, and the lips turn grey and dry. Be aware, though, that this paling of the skin man also be explained by *anaemia*: meaning "without blood", this is a condition in which there is a lack of red blood cells. The symptoms mirror those of a suspected vampire attack, namely a greying pallor, lethargy and light-headedness.

UNEXPLAINED DEATH: Vampires are often blamed for the sudden death of otherwise healthy people. Such inexplicable fatalities are doubly suspicious if the victim dies within a few days of the burial of a close relative.

FATIGUE: Just as the vampire bat slowly sucks the life from its prey, returning repeatedly over a period of days, weeks, or even months, so too may the revenant feed methodically, night after night, draining unsuspecting victims of blood or energy. Anyone complaining of inexplicable weariness, dizziness, lethargy or exhaustion is under suspicion of vampiric attack.

Of course, this may simply be tiredness, or the result of an undiagnosed illness. However, you should not rule out the effects of nightly psychic attacks on the body. Psychic vampirism – and the unwanted attention from succubi and incubi – may be assaults on the energy centres of the mind or body, but the effects will also take their toll on the physical body.

Finally, those who unwittingly provide a meal for the revenant may appear malnourished: as the vampire feeds, its prey becomes increasingly skeletal, wasting away until death, at which point he or she may return as a vampire.

Victims of vampire attacks are sometimes thought to join the ranks of the undead. Anyone displaying common vampire signs may be "on the turn". Action must be taken before or upon death to prevent them returning as "real" vampires.

† Protection from the Undead

The Spanish, French and Italians all consider Saturday the luckiest day of the week

Some vampires can only be conquered at certain times: e.g. the German neuntöter can only be staked between 11 pm and midnight

IF YOUR INVESTIGATION of a village or town unearths the unmistakable manifestations of vampirism, you will want to locate the source of the problem as soon as possible. But before you head off into the night with your sharpened stakes, prepare yourself amply for an encounter with the undead.

Think first about when you should begin your vampire hunt. For example, many Christian countries regard Saturday as the day most sacred to the Virgin Mary, and the time when evil is at its least mischievous. In Greece, the *vrykolakas* sleeps only on a Saturday, so there is no better time to run it through with a stake, and witches will choose any day but a Saturday for their Sabbaths. To the Greeks, those born on a Saturday – "Sabbatarians" – are believed to be blessed with heightened psychic senses and an innate ability to sniff out the undead. Some Sabbatarians are partnered with equally sensitive dogs; others wield a degree of power over the undead and can force the vampire to act against its will.

The time of day is also of great importance to the hunter. Vampire fiction has taught us that the undead only walk the earth by night,

and there is sufficient evidence in folklore for this to be taken seriously. A beast that hunts under the cover of darkness will, by dawn, be replete and bloated with blood. In this torpid state, its movements will be sluggish, making it easier prey. Take your cue from the crowing of the cockerel.

However, not all vampires are restricted to night. Daywalkers, as they are known, are those species of vampire that can roam when they choose. The *upior* of Poland, for instance, rises daily at noon and spends the next twelve hours greedily feasting on as much blood as its barbed tongue can lap up. A Russian relative of the *upior*, the iron-toothed *upyr*, also stirs between noon and midnight, when it hunts down and consumes the juicy flesh of children.

Protection

Before embarking on a vampire hunt, consider the steps necessary to protect yourself. The devout slayer will find spiritual protection from the Bible; some may lighten their load simply by carrying with them the first fourteen verses of the Gospel of St John. The efficacy of such items is – as always – determined by the faith placed in them.

Religious icons and amulets – such as the seal of St Benedict – provide similar security, as do necklaces and brooches bearing a crucifix or Calvary cross.

Latin translations:

CSSML = May the Holy Cross for me be a light

NDSMD = Let not the Dragon be my guide

CSPB = The Cross of the Holy Father Benedict

VRSNSMV = Begone Satan; suggest not to me thy vain things

SMQLIVB = The drink you offer is evil; drink that poison yourself

PAX = peace

69

Evil Eye charm from Greece

Wouldn't recommend consuming blood at all!

The Igbo people of southern Nigeria wear a protective bracelet that binds the soul to the body and thus prevents an evil spirit taking possession, while the Malayans wear black silk armbands when at risk from psychic attack. The vampire hunters of Russia and India protect themselves with a splash of chicken blood. The bird must first be killed next to the body of a vampire's victim, then the blood used to anoint the hunter's face. From Prussia comes another form of blood offering: drinking the blood of the victim of a vampire mixed with some brandy. Similarly, the Poles place their faith in "blood bread" or "blood cakes". These small patties are baked with the blood of a suspected vampire, and are said to provide immunity from vampire attacks.

Finally, you should arm yourself with the standard weapons of the vampire hunter (*see pages 114–17*), and carry them with you at all times in a sturdy kitbag. As far as clothing is concerned, particularly pious hunters will swear by the cilice, or haircloth – the coarse goat's-hair shirt usually worn as a penance. But although some may draw spiritual strength from such asceticism, for most others the cloth is felt to be too abrasive. The practical vampire hunter is therefore advised to opt for a comfortable suit of a material sufficiently durable to withstand the ravages of thorny thickets and muddy cemeteries.

Other means of protection:

- *Tiger's-tooth necklace*
- *Brass finger ring*
- *Sprig of hawthorn or some such thorny plant in your lapel*
- *Splash yourself with garlic oil or holy water*
- *Crescent-shaped charms: boar tusks, pieces of coral, a horseshoe, chicken wish bone*

If all else fails, prayer!

FIGURE 15

A GARLAND OF GARLIC IS THE CLASSIC VAMPIRE REPELLENT — WHETHER WORN AROUND THE NECK, SUSPENDED OVER THE THRESHOLD OR SLUNG AROUND THE NECK OF A POTENTIALLY VAMPIRIC CORPSE.

Hunting with Animals

"They select a young lad who is a pure maiden – that is to say, who, as they believe, had never performed the sexual act. He is set up upon a young stallion who has not yet mounted his first mare, who has never stumbled, and who must be coal-black without a speck of white; the stud is ridden into the cemetery in and out among the graves and that grave over which the steed in spite of blows they deal him pretty handsomely refuses to pass is where the Vampire lies."

The Returned, *Dom Augustin Calmet, (1746)*

In Germany, if a woman uses a horse collar to ease the pain of childbirth, the child is likely to become a vampire

FEW CREATURES ARE SPARED the unwanted curse of the vampire: throughout the world, vampire lore is littered with tales of howling wolves, bloodthirsty bats and demonic black dogs all indentured to the undead. But animals are not exclusively the slaves of the Devil. Indeed, when hunting the undead, animals may be among your greatest allies.

Horses

In Albania, our equine allies are employed as vampire hunters, and in Scotland the cloven-hoofed, bloodsucking *baobhan-sith* is terrified of horses. Be aware, however, that not all species of vampire are afraid of horses. The Japanese *kappa* will hungrily exsanguinate a horse, sucking the warm blood from its anus, while the Russian *upyr* and Indian *vetala* both ride a horse, the latter being recognized by its livid green coat.

Dogs

For reliability, obedience and companionship, the vampire slayer is advised to befriend a dog. With their heightened senses and loyalty to their master, dogs can not only protect you from the undead, but also sniff them out and frighten them away.

Vampire hunters in the Caribbean will already know of the dog's uncanny ability to detect a vampire. Indeed, in these tropical climes, anyone on the receiving end of the bark or snarl of a dog is immediately suspected of paying obeisance to Satan.

At the heels of the Greek Sabbatarians (*see page 68*) you may see (or, indeed, be *unable* to see) a "fetch dog". These companion spirits aid Sabbatarians in their fight against the undead, and can take any form – although the dog is the most common. A similar form of spirit pet, the *fylgia*, exists in Iceland, where such creatures accompany and protect their human master for a lifetime.

Wolves

Finally, where you find vampires you are also likely to find wolves. These "children of the night", as Bram Stoker's eponymous Count refers to them, should not always be feared: throughout most of Europe, at least, wolves prey upon the undead, prowling protectively around cemeteries and devouring anything that might rise from its grave. Of course, in some other parts of the world, they are also linked with the dreaded werewolf. I leave you to make the correct judgement, but recommend in both cases keeping a respectable distance.

Animal guardians are common throughout the world: Totemism in the Americas and animal familiars in American and Russian Shamanic cultures

† Using Dhampirs

ONE OF THE MORE fascinating characters in vampire mythology – and one rarely seized upon by the writers of vampire literature – is the dhampir, the offspring of a vampire.

According to Gypsy lore from Eastern Europe, the undead soul – or *mullo* – is first and foremost the servant of his loins. Driven by an insatiable lust for his widow, he will visit her on his first night out of the grave and conceive with her a child that is half vampire, half human. This dhampir grows up torn between its vampire-like lust for blood and its desire to be normal. As it matures, it develops a hatred and bitterness towards its vampire father; it also acquires a range of supernatural powers, including control over animals, superhuman strength and, most importantly, the ability to detect the undead.

Dhampirs are driven by the need for revenge against their Satanic sires, which – along with their ability to daywalk – makes them greatly prized as vampire hunters. Revenants otherwise invisible to us mortals will appear as flesh and blood to the dhampir, who can destroy them in a fight or "kill" them with a single gunshot.

Finding a dhampir is not easy; finding a *genuine* dhampir is harder still. Many Gypsy charlatans will lay claim to a vampiric heritage, charging small fortunes to eradicate villages of their supposed vampire infestations. They will wrestle "invisible" foes and perform elaborate ceremonies with much whistling and dervish-like whirling. Do not be fooled: if confronted by such mountebankery, ask for demonstration of strength – lifting a horse or pushing down a tree, for example.

In certain regions of Europe, dhampirs were thought to have jelly-like bodies and a very short lifespan. In other areas, it was known that dhampirs lived full and normal lives, even passing on their vampiric essence through their bloodline and bequeathing supernatural powers to their children.

Although they may possess incredible strength, dhampirs are not invincible. Once dead they will remain dead.

The last dhampir ceremony I've heard of took place as recently as 1959, in Vrbica, Kossvo

Beware of imitations! Charlatan dhampirs – or dhampires – will perform bizarre rituals such as wearing their clothes inside out or using their inside-out coatsleeves as "vampire telescopes"!!!

Other dhampir names:
- *Dhampir*
- *Lampijerovic*
- *Vampir*
- *Vampuiera*

"Little Vampires"

† Cemeteries

FIGURE 16
THE CEMETERY: THE
PLACE OF REST WHERE
THE VAMPIRE SLAYER,
CONVERSELY, MAY FIND
NO REST. OBTAIN A
MUNICIPAL MAP OF LOCAL
GRAVEYARDS AND WALK
EVERY INCH UNTIL YOU
KNOW EACH TWIST AND
TURN. THIS IS YOUR
HUNTING GROUND.

COMMON SENSE DICTATES that the search for that which you cannot find begins in the last place you saw it. So where better to start your search for the undead than in a cemetery?

Despite a usual abundance of cruciform monuments – and a scarcity of living, breathing food – the graveyard is a vampire's most likely habitat. Mausolea, tombs, catacombs and burial chambers provide not only shelter and security to the undead but also protection from the rays of the sun so deadly to many forms of vampire.

There are two main types of burial ground. The first is the graveyard – a plot of land often adjoining or encircling a church, and attended to by a sexton (with whom the vampire hunter should always try to strike up a friendship). Such grounds may accommodate a few humble plots or a vast network of graves, and may also house mausolea.

The second type of burial ground is the municipal cemetery. In the nineteenth century, an exodus of workers from the countryside to the town – and a heavy increase in battlefield deaths – meant that church graveyards could no longer accommodate the dead. The solution was the creation of large garden graveyards on the outskirts of towns, or fields reserved for the bodies of fallen war heroes.

Some vampires never travel beyond their cemetery walls. This is particularly the case in India, where the *bhuta*, *rakshasa* and *pacu pati* vampires all prefer to make their homes in the trees and bushes of burial grounds. Here, the bloodthirsty revenants can feast on the organs of their fellow deceased, gnawing through skulls to eat the brains or sucking excreta from the bowels and intestines.

The vampire hunter's aim, of course, is to discover and dispatch the bloodsuckers while they sleep. For this reason, the best time to investigate a cemetery is during the day – preferably on a Saturday, when evil activity is traditionally at its minimum. A walk around a graveyard can also be useful in identifying the graves of potential vampires, who can be dealt with before they even leave their coffins.

Beg, borrow or steal the coat from a municipal grave digger: you can pass through the cemetery with shovels and tools without looking too suspicious

Legal issues

Vampire hunters can be charged with the following offences:

- Being in an enclosed area for an unlawful purpose
- Interfering with remains
- Malicious damage to tombs and coffins
- Offending religion, decency and morality

✝ The hunter should look for some or all of the following classic signs of vampire activity.

DISTURBED EARTH: A vampire rising from its grave will obviously disturb the earth as it claws its way up through the soil. Look for areas of broken earth, mounds of mud and footprints in the soil leading away from the fissure.

EXSANGUINATED CORPSES: Vampires will feed on any living creature if hungry enough, so the discovery of the bodies of rodents and small animals drained of blood is a sign that a revenant may be active. If possible, retain a corpse for later investigation.

DISTURBED ANIMALS: In some parts of Europe, animals are led through cemeteries in search of the undead. Horses are considered the most sensitive of creatures and will not cross the grave of a vampire. Certain areas require that a virgin be riding bareback; others that the horse is jet black. Black dogs, black crows and white wolves are also keen vampire hunters.

From the Greek for "wild beast" – having the ability to take on animal form

(Note: take great care that you do not use an animal that is, in fact, a theriomorphic vampire, as it will most likely turn on you.)

SIGNS OF FORCED EXIT: Investigate for signs of damage to mausolea, tombs and catacombs. Some vampires are known to have supernatural strength and can tear apart chains with ease. Note that shape-shifting vampires can more easily leave a burial chamber by taking on the form of an animal – spiders, bats, rats and snakes are common – or even a mist.

No birdsong in the cemetery? A vampire could be resident.

DAMAGED COFFINS: In underground catacombs, examine the loculi – the individual units each housing a coffin – for signs of disturbance. Expect coffin lids to have been prised or pushed off (check for claw marks on the underside). Remember, however, that many types of vampire may return to the same coffin each night. To prevent this, scatter garlic (cloves or oil) inside the coffin, or lay out pieces of consecrated host in a cross shape.

BOILING SOIL: A drop of holy water or garlic oil over the grave of a vampire will cause the earth to hiss and burn. In such cases, push a wooden stake into the soil to impale the creature as it attempts to leave.

FIGURE 17

THE LID OF A STONE SARCOPHAGUS LIES AJAR, EVIDENCE, PERHAPS, OF A STIRRING REVENANT. LOOK FOR FOOTPRINTS HEADING AWAY FROM SUCH OPENED GRAVES.

FINGER-SIZED HOLES: Non-corporeal vampires have been witnessed leaving their graves in the form of mist. This demonic vapour issues from thin, finger-thick holes that the keen vampire hunter may see in the soil.

† Charnel Houses

In Poland, burial plots are rented for 40 years at a time – after that, you're dug up and put in storage

FIGURE 18

THE SKELETAL REMAINS LEFT TO ROT AT THE CHARNEL HOUSE PROVIDE AMPLE COVER TO THE REVENANT. ENTER ONLY WITH A STRONG RESOLVE – AND WELL-SHARPENED STAKE.

AT THE START of the nineteenth century, before the widespread use of cemeteries, church graveyards suffered from enormous overcrowding. Not wishing to refuse money for burials, clerics would cram their graveyards, burying body on top of body. Indeed, arms and legs could regularly be seen sticking up from the earth, providing a generous supper for hungry animals. During outbreaks of the plague, cholera and other epidemics, families coming to pay their respects to the dead put themselves at further risk of infection.

The short-term solution was the charnel house, or ossuary. After a specified period of time, the dead would be disinterred and their remains kept in a building or vault designed to store the bones of the dead. The charnel house – from the Latin *carnalis*, "relating to flesh" – freed up burial space, but still allowed families to pay their respects.

Some of the larger charnel houses took on

the air of ornate, baroque cathedrals. The
bones would be arranged ornamentally over
walls, pillars and doors, forming both a tasteful
monument and a chilling *memento mori*.
Others, however, became a poor relative of the
graveyard. Without the money to pay for a
funeral, families would often send their
deceased directly to the charnel, where they
would be left to rot or be picked over by the
local rodent population. Some unscrupulous
patriarchs would sometimes promise burials
but have the corpses dug up and dumped in the
charnel house almost immediately, making way
for more fee-paying arrivals.

These rotting, feculent slums – dumping
ground for the unbaptized, the unclaimed, the
insane and the apostate – therefore constitute
an ideal breeding ground for revenants. Here,
the undead relish the disease, the decay and the
darkness, and there are few places where you
more likely to encounter vampires. Be warned,
however: the smell is usually unbearable.

Carry before you a thurible of burning
incense on any visit to a charnel house. This
will not only deter the undead but sweeten the
air. You would also be advised to wear a mask
covering your nose and mouth. A sprinkler or
atomizer of holy water will assist in keeping any
bloodsuckers at bay, and help you identify
potential vampires slumbering among the
bones and viscera.

Must visit Church of San Bernardino in Milan – looks beautiful!

A cycling mask offers some protection – and burn a joss stick if you can't find any incense (plus: two joss sticks make a pretty good cross in an emergency)

† Morgues and Hospitals

JUST AS BLOOD is the very essence of life, so too is it the essence of undeath. For, without its powerful association with blood, vampire lore would be as redundant or as anachronistic as that of faerie or spiritualism. By draining the living of such a vital fluid, the vampire has become an influential archetype, securing everlasting life in more ways than one.

The significance of blood goes beyond its role of carrying oxygen and carbon dioxide around the body. It is both the giver of life and a measure of our strength. To lose blood is to lose our power, which is why it comes to us as no surprise that the vampire should seek to drink our vital blood and rejuvenate his own decaying flesh.

A refreshing mouthful of revitalizing blood need not be sucked from the neck of a hapless virgin. The pragmatic revenant will seek out his food from hospitals – although ill health may affect the quality of blood, the victims are likely to offer less resistance. Expect to find them, too, in sanatoria and even morgues.

But remember that not all vampires need blood: some are happy with human flesh and even rotting viscera or faeces. Others will make

In 1492, a Hebrew physician paid a ducat each for the blood of three young men in their prime in order to revitalize the ailing Pope Innocent VIII

Find out where the hospital sends its clinical waste, as the hungry vampire might follow. Also, check out local blood bank – ask if anyone has been making unsolicited job applications.

a meal of animals. Anywhere you find the infirm or dying, you may also find a vampire, so erase the fictional image of the charismatic, seductive aristocrat: you are more likely to seek a desperate creature hunting for its next meal.

> *Seen anyone suspicious hanging around the local vet or animal welfare shelter? What about the pet shop?*

HAIR AND ITS MYSTERIOUS PROPERTIES

The Malay vampire hunter uses a length of iron pipe and a cut-throat razor to identify his prey. When he suspects he is in the vicinity of a vampire, he draws the razor over the iron, at which point the revenant's hair falls out as if cut with the blade, clearly identifying him.

Hair also plays a part in the hunting of the beautiful but deadly Malay *langsuir*. One of the few guaranteed ways to revoke her power is to trim her ankle-length hair and pare her fingernails.

> *Like the story of Samson: his strength is in his hair*

Hair and – to a lesser extent – fingernails have always been connected to life and the spirit. The Maori cast spells while having their hair cut, while the Karo-Bataks and Toradjas consider the hair the repository of the soul. Moslem men still leave a single tuft of hair unshaved on their heads to help Mohammed pluck them from earth and lift them to Paradise; and in one Fijian tribe, the chief would even eat a fellow tribesman each time his hair was cut, lest he expose his soul to evil.

> *In some Thai hair-cutting ceremonies, cords are tied round the waist to prevent the soul escaping*

83

† Churches, Castles and Remote Places

FIGURE 19
ENGRAVING (1875)
REPRODUCED IN SPANISH
MAGAZINE *La Ilustración
Espanola y Americana*.
THE DESERTED CASTLE
REPRESENTS THE CLASSIC
IMAGE OF THE ABOMINABLE
BEAST'S ABODE: GRAND,
GOTHIC, ISOLATED AND
INACCESSIBLE.

THE POPULARITY of Bram Stoker's *Dracula* has ensured that our mind's eye sees the vampire as a reclusive gent living in a remote hilltop castle fanned by beating bat wings and surrounded by baying wolves. Indeed, Castle Dracula, Stoker's inspiration for his imaginary Count's abode, is an imposing, lonely palace 1,500 feet above the Arges River.

However, from what we have learned about real vampires, it is most unlikely that you will find a revenant in his own cliff-side citadel or isolated fortress. Of course, if there happens to be an abandoned castle close to an outbreak of vampirism, then make it the first stop in your investigation – anywhere impenetrable enough to keep visitors away is a potential lair.

Most abandoned buildings – if suitably isolated – offer some form of protection for the vampire. Those far from the sea or flowing rivers, and those that receive little in the way of sunlight, are particularly suspect. With your slayer's kit at the ready (*see pages 114–17*), be prepared to inspect old theatres, hospitals, warehouses and mine tunnels for signs of activity. Expect to find:–

~ ANIMAL bones picked clean of meat
~ COFFINS with a thin layer of soil inside
~ A STRANGE-ACTING or pale caretaker
~ BOARDED-UP windows
~ A LACK OF plants and vegetation
~ UNBEARABLE stench of death and decay
~ UNIDENTIFIABLE body parts
~ VICIOUS black guard dogs
~ FREEZING cold temperatures

Consecrated ground does not appear to cause the Satanic revenant any discomfort. Many revenants have been witnessed rising and returning from graves in the grounds of churches, so even *they* may harbour the undead. However, given the undoubted preference of the vampire for all things unholy, it is perhaps arguable that they are more likely to be found on deconsecrated property.

Signs of vampire activity in churches:

• Desecrated religious symbols
• Broken cruciform monuments
• Smashed stained-glass windows
• Absence of candles
• Evidence of black magic (inverted pentagrams, chicken feathers, dead cats)

Beware of trespass laws — you're no use in jail!

† forests and Swamps

AMPIRES SEEK OUT the feculent and foul, so you may need to search beyond the cemetery or castle walls and investigate the more "natural" habitats of the undead.

FORESTS: Trees provide a surprising number of vampire species with nesting space. Among the tree-dwellers are:

Langsuir (Malaya): Often taking the form of an owl with large, hideous claws, this female fiend perches in trees or on the roof of its potential victim. It may be distinguished from a normal owl by its demonic screeching. The *pontianak* is the stillborn child of a *langsuir*, and also exists at night as a tree-dwelling owl.

Asanbosam (Africa): Deep in the forest lives this iron-toothed monster. Nestling in the branches of trees, it swings its great talon-like feet into the path of passers-by, who are scooped up to become the creature's next meal.

Loogaroo (Grenada): This witch-vampire uses the silk-cotton tree (*Bombax ceiba*, or Devil's tree) as a secret hiding place for its skin, which it sheds at night before going about its ghastly business. Should you find the skin, shower it with salt.

Baital (India): Sometimes seen astride a green horse, this chief of Indian demons inhabits trees and can take on a number of different forms, including that of a repulsive old woman.

Yara-ma-yha-who (Australia): Found in the fig trees, these vampires swing down to attack passers-by, draining their blood through suckers on their fingers.

CAVES: The vampire bat is by no means the only bloodsucker to be found during the day in the dark safety of a cave. Dank, uninhabited and usually remote, fissures in the rock or natural underground chambers make a good resting place for the undead. The *bantu* of India, for example, makes its home in such places. Certain sub-species enslave dogs to hunt for food on their behalf.

Beware of vampiric flies and mosquitoes, or other malevolent insects – they may be under the control of Satan, Lord of the Flies

SWAMPS: Thick with choking vapours and stinking marsh gas, sewers and swamps are a likely habitat for the vampire. Indeed, will-o'-the-wisps – the phosphorescent, gaseous orbs seen over marshes – were once considered the spectral remnants of the dead.

Don't forget the anti-mosquito spray!!

✝

CHAPTER 4

Preventing Vampires

Prevention is always better than cure. To deny the vampire the opportunity to rise, take all steps necessary while the "deceased" remains warm.

IN CULTURES that regard the death of the physical body as a transitional phase, the dissolution of the corpse is considered vital if the spirit is to ascend to the next life. Such beliefs are reflected in the funerary rites. In Tibet, for example, it is believed that birds carry the soul of the deceased to the afterlife, so a corpse is given an "air burial", in which it is dismembered and left on an open piece of land to be picked at by the waiting vultures.

Similarly, in Persia I have seen Parsee dead, left as carrion atop a "tower of silence" – a type of funerary mound with a pit to receive the picked bones. Furthermore, the Australian Aborigines leave their dead in trees before offering the rank, half-eaten remains to the ants; only then are the bones treated with reverence and buried.

Other races, such as the ancient Egyptians and the pre-Inca Andean cultures, believed in a somatic death – that is, an afterlife in which the integrity of the physical body was of paramount importance. This resulted in a wide range of complex funerary customs that involved embalming, mummification and oblations to preserve and appease the dead.

Offering of food / flowers etc to appease God or the dead

Despite these two contrary positions, the consequences of not following the appropriate funeral rites were the same: spiritual unrest and the increased risk of vampirism.

If you should suspect that a man or woman will return as a vampire, there are a number of precautions you can take before, upon or soon after death. These safeguards take many forms – physical or symbolic – but all are intended to curtail or prevent entirely the reanimation of the body.

ABSOLUTION: The Church may be the first recourse in preventing vampirism, especially if the deceased has died excommunicate or apostate. A simple ceremony of absolution may be enough to end the curse of vampirism.

OBSEQUIES: The manner in which the body is treated after death has implications for its passage in the afterlife. In some cultures, a deep burial may be sufficient to prevent the return of the dead, while in others only total dismemberment, cremation or embalming will guarantee the finality of death. No matter

Funeral rites

✝ how barbaric or alien such practices are, a funeral that conforms to social and religious convention is considered "clean", and should always be considered before resorting to more physical – or violent – methods.

OFFERINGS: Sacrifices and oblations may also appease the dead and provide protection from demoniacal spirits, particularly if offered on feast days. In such ceremonies, the dead are symbolically nourished with specially prepared food and drink.

BINDING: The suspicious corpse can be restrained – again, physically or symbolically – thus limiting fiendish movements post-mortem. Precautions may range from simply tightening the winding sheet to pinning the body to the earth with a stake.

MUTILATION: A step further is the maiming of the corpse to prevent movement. By depriving the vampire of anything from its tendons to its head, you are effectively "killing" the creature before it is "born". Cremation is, of course, the ultimate form of mutilation.

Absolution

Before we begin maiming or disinterring corpses, it is worth investigating the status of the deceased in the eyes of the Church. Has he or she been excommunicated? If this form of ecclesiastical censure is deemed to be one of the prime causes of vampirism, then clearly the first course of action must be to have the ban lifted.

I have heard tales of vampires crumbling to dust as soon as a bishop or priest has uttered the last word of an absolution. These may yet be fantastical yarns circulated by the faithful to prove Christianity the one true religion, but the relatively clean and simple process of lifting this ban should be investigated.

Find a cleric of the necessary stature to deliver the absolution. If none is forthcoming, consider making a small "donation" to the Church, for it is not unknown for the families of dead excommunicates to buy the path of their loved one back into the Church.

You should also be aware, also, that those who die apostate – that is, those who choose while living to forsake the Church – are also deemed excommunicate, and may also need absolution. Indeed, anyone who dies under the spell of a curse (ecclesiastical or otherwise) will need some form of liberty if they are not to return as the undead.

Exorcism, or some other form of cleansing rite, should also be considered, although this course of action will require you to seek out the services of an experienced priest with the power to cast out unclean spirits.

"And when he had called unto him his twelve disciples, he gave them the power against unclean spirits, to cast them out"

Matthew 10, 1

† Specific Burial Practices

Burial

THE PROPER HANDLING and (inhumation) of the deceased is, in many cultures, enough to prevent vampirism. In parts of Europe, for example, custom dictates that a coffin removed from a house should be carried out head first – and without touching the threshold – lest a demonic spirit seize control of the body. On the other side of the world in China, a moonbeam is enough to transform the spirit of the dead into a vampiric *chiang-shi*, so a body must not be left exposed in the open for any length of time.

As we have already seen, animals should be kept away from the deceased at all costs. In Scotland, it is customary to lock up all pets between a death and the funeral, and throughout Europe it is assumed that if an animal leaps over a corpse – or a bird flies overhead – the departing soul will enter the beast and assume control, leaving the "empty" corpse at risk from diabolical possession.

Death Plugs
Placing certain objects in the coffin or on the corpse is thought to ensure the safe journey of the soul, and prevent a vampire from taking possession of the corpse. These can range

from seasonal fruits to religious icons. But perhaps the most enduring of these customs is the depositing of "freight money" or "passage money". Silver coins are placed over the eyes or mouth to pay Charon, the ferryman of the River Styx. According to classical mythology, failure to pay the ferryman results in an eternity spent on the edge of Limbo being stung repeatedly by wasps.

However, I believe that this is a modern, aetiological explanation for the practice, the origins of which have been lost in the mists of time. Uneducated peasants unaware of Greek

And when we sneeze, the soul might escape, which is why we say "God bless you"

"The Dead in Love"

FIGURE 20

COLOURED LITHOGRAPH (1857) ILLUSTRATING A CLANDESTINE BURIAL FROM THÉOPHILE GAUTIER'S VAMPIRE TALE *La Morte Amoureuse* (1836).

or Roman mythologies would seal the lips or eyes of their dead with anything from coins and wax to shards of pottery and handfuls of earth.

The more likely explanation is that the eyes and mouth are considered a portal through which a soul leaves or enters the body. Today, we talk of our eyes as the windows on our soul, and we still cover our mouths when we yawn: originally this was done not out of politeness but to prevent the Devil from entering. So by covering the eyes and mouth (and any other orifice) with such items, we prevent a demonic spirit entering the corpse and using it for its Satanic ends.

Religious Relics and Artefacts

There is a religious precedent for this symbolic sealing of the lips. Priests have been known to place a Eucharist particle (a wafer of consecrated host) on the lips of the deceased, or in the coffin, to prevent vampirism. It was considered profane, however, to place the host on the body of a known vampire, for whom absolution or a swift decapitation was the only acceptable cure.

Also placed on the lips are potsherds. These are pieces of earthenware often etched with "I X NI KA", meaning "Jesus Christ Conquers". Whether these are intended to seal the mouth or provide the revenant with a readily available meal is unclear, but it is nevertheless a worthwhile precaution.

Bees were once thought to come directly from heaven, which is why wax candles are so associated with churches. In Russia, corpses are buried with candles to illuminate the path to heaven.

Etched or painted on the potsherd might be a pentagram, the mystical five-pointed star. This ancient symbol, found on pottery from the earliest of Mesopotamian civilizations (c.5000 BC), has always been associated with good fortune. Later, it was chosen by the Church to symbolize, variously, the five wounds of Christ, the five books of the Pentateuch and the five virtues. The strength of the pentagram lies ultimately in the faith of the beholder, so with the confidence that such a symbol bestows, wear a pentagram amulet around the neck, or daub a five-pointed star on a doorway or cowshed to bar the entry of any malign spirit.

Also, sealing the lips of the deceased with wax – especially that from a paschal candle melted between Holy Saturday and Pentecost – is all the more effective when impressed with a pentagram.

Consider, too, the ancient Jewish custom of clasping together the hands of the dead. The fingers of the corpse would be arranged in such a way to form the Hebrew word for God, thus offering the corpse invincible protection from possession by Satan or his minions.

Deathly Distractions

Objects may also be placed in the coffin to keep the undead occupied upon awakening. A snarl of knotted string or wool – or a tangled

Magical pentagram

The point-down or inverted pentagram has been adopted in the 20th century as a symbol of Satanism and black magic. Be careful to draw only a point-up pentagram

Remember: finger rings are thought to bind the soul to the body, so remove before burial

fishnet – will keep the beast busy as it unravels the threads at the rate of one per year. Seeds scattered into the coffin and over the body will perform the same task (*see page 130*).

Another useful form of distraction involves removing just one of the socks of the suspected vampire. Just as a revenant is driven to distraction by knots and seeds, so too will it become obsessed with its missing sock; until the sock is back on its foot, the vampire will be unable to fulfil its foul passions. For added impact, fill the sock with garlic and pitch it into a fast-running stream.

In Pomerania, a songbook is traditionally buried with the suspected vampire to keep it amused, and in Romania a bottle of whisky by the side of the deceased will prevent the *strigoii* from forming. I have also been reassured that drinking wine that has been buried with a corpse for six weeks provides ample protection from any bloodsucker.

In the Ground

The burial of a suspected vampire in a grave twice as deep as usual is often considered sufficient, although there are some additional precautions that can be taken. Throughout the Greek islands, suspected vampires are buried (or reinterred) on remote, uninhabited islets, as revenants cannot cross salt water. In other parts of Europe, the dead are buried prone –

facing downwards in the coffin. The ravenous vampire instinctively claws its way to the surface in search of food, but buried prone it awakens disorientated and instead digs itself deeper and deeper into the earth.

Prone burial also helps to ensure that the eyes of the deceased do not fall on a mourner, which in some cultures is enough to result in vampirism.

Re China: if a vampire has left its grave, leave the lid off the coffin – the fresh air is enough to purify it and prevent the vampire from returning

What about the Chinese Cemetery in Manila? This necropolis has mausolea many storeys high, some with bathrooms, kitchens and bedrooms. Some have even got air conditioning and karaoke machines!

✝ Cremation

"Dust thou art, and unto dust thou shalt return"

Genesis 3, 19

CREMATION IS WITHOUT QUESTION the most effective means of destroying a vampire. It is also one of the most difficult, expensive and controversial.

The burning of the dead has been practised sporadically throughout the world since the early Stone Age. However, the entombment of Christ and his subsequent resurrection set a precedent in the West.

Many Christians risked their lives to ensure that the saints and martyrs received a Christian burial, while pagans attempted to destroy faith in the resurrection by digging them up and burning them. Those who committed the flesh to the fire were eventually considered enemies of the Catholic faith, despite neither the Old nor New Testament proscribing it. By the fall of Roman Empire, cremation was considered throughout most of the world to be barbaric and pagan.

It was only with the 1873 Vienna Exposition, and the appearance of Snr Brunetti's modern cremation apparatus, that conflagration became financially viable – not to mention, once again, a Christian concern. Offended by what appeared to be a "public profession of irreligion and materialism", the Catholic Church banned cremations in 1886.

Ban lifted in 1963

The Hindus, of course, choose to cremate their dead, burning the bodies on impressive open pyres and casting the "cremains" into water. The Ganges, India's most sacred river, offers cosmic regeneration and accepts tons of ashes and calcified bones from partially burned bodies.

Practicalities

Should you resort to vampire cremation in a Christian county, be aware of interference from others. The clergy may insist on administering what they regard to be the appropriate rites. Police, municipal notaries and the family of the deceased may also hinder your work.

You must be aware of the amount of wood required for a cremation. You will also need a decent amount of readily combustible material (such as straw or linen) to act as kindling, and must keep about your person matches, flint or steel ignition. Once the blaze is under way, be aware of animals – rodents, insects and birds – that might escape from a conflagration. Should a single soul escape the flames, the vampire may transfer to a new body.

The ashes from a vampire cremation should be swept up into a sack and hurled into fast-flowing water. This prevents any initiate of black magic using the remains for evil. You may also find it prudent to disinter and cremate bodies from plots adjacent to the original vampire.

"Need Fires"
Cattle herds suspected of being under attack from a vampire are driven between two large ceremonial pyres, the smoke and flames from which purge the beasts of their affliction

99

† Mutilation

FIGURE 21
SIXTEENTH-CENTURY
WOODCUT DEPICTING THE
DECAPITATION OF PETER
STUBBE, A SUSPECTED
LYCANTHROPE. THE DEFT
REMOVAL OF THE UNDEAD'S
HEAD PROVIDES A SWIFT
AND SURE END TO THEIR
TORMENT.

A STEP BEYOND BINDING, corpse mutilation is an unpleasant and undignified practice that may be nonetheless necessary to prevent the rise of the diabolical fiend.

The degree of mutilation necessary will depend on the severity of the vampire epidemic or of the strength of the revenant. Pre-burial procedures such as stitching the mouth, hammering a nail through the skull, piercing the heart or even crippling the beast by severing its hamstrings or breaking its legs may be enough. You may, however, discover that more drastic measures must be taken.

Decapitation is the most common form of mutilation. For this, a sexton's spade should suffice, although an axe is a useful addition to the vampire slayer's kit (*see pages 114–17*). It is usually sufficient to place the severed head between the feet of the vampire or under the

body, so long as cloves of garlic are used to plug the wounds.

As an additional measure, vampire slayers have been known to bury the head elsewhere, throw it into a river, cremate it or boil it in oil.

During the most severe vampire epidemics, it will be necessary for bodies to be disinterred, dismembered, hacked into small pieces and then cremated. Some insist on taking things further still: in Greece, suspected vampires are disinterred and then boiled in holy water, holy oil or wine before being returned to the grave.

Finally, the internal organs – particularly the heart – may also be wrenched from the body and destroyed. You might consider following the example of the Serbian vampire hunter, who boils the heart in vinegar, burns it to ash and spoons the powdery residue back into the cavity.

**MUMMIFICATION:
THE ULTIMATE PROTECTION?**

Sophisticated embalming techniques that were developed in Ancient Egypt have enabled the shell of a corpse to be preserved for centuries. This process also guaranteed the body protection from vampirism.

Firstly, the brain was removed using a barbed hook forced repeatedly up through the nose. The abdomen was then slit and eviscerated of all but the heart; the excised organs were treated with preservatives – which would prove to offer little in the way of protection – and stored in a Canopic vase.

Secondly, the body cavity was cleaned and filled with resins, perfumes and myrrh – all of which are known vampire repellents.

Finally, after a long bath in saltpetre, the body was perfumed once again and wound tightly in layer upon layer of linen bandages, thus forming a binding that guaranteed immobility to the restless undead.

I remember one case where a body was hacked into pieces and fed to stray dogs and pigeons

† Restricting the Corpse

EXCEPT FOR ITS CLIMB out of the grave – the explanation for which largely eludes us – the corporeal vampire is more or less as restricted in its movements as any living person. This has led over the last few hundred years to a wide selection of preventative measures to ensure that the revenant cannot escape its final resting place.

Perhaps the most obvious and literal restriction is the stake. By pounding a wooden stake through the chest or heart of a corpse, you are effectively pinning the physical body to the earth – and, as we will discover later, there is also a symbolic element to this act. Similarly, large nails can be used to secure the body to the casket, as practised by the Finnish *chuwashé* (or *chuvashia)*. However, there are other, more subtle (and certainly less messy) methods that can be employed to prevent a vampire leaving its grave.

Consider weighing down the corpse, either literally by placing rocks or a stone slab on the chest, or symbolically using religious items or a garland made of one (or some) of the many powerful natural plants known to repulse the undead (*see pages 106–9*). Push stones into the mouth of the corpse and tie the jaw closed with bands of linen. If the deceased is not already a

vampire, the stones will prevent a malign spirit
entering the body; if it has already undergone
its transformation, it will give the revenant
something to chew on should it indulge in the
diabolical *mandicatione mortuorum*.

    In Ireland, I have witnessed one particular
burial in which stones were piled high on top of
the grave to prevent the deceased clawing its
way out. In many parts of the world, stones are
piled on the graves of suicides – in parts of
Africa and the Middle East it is not uncommon
to see passers-by throwing stones at the graves
of suicides or wrong-doers. The Baganda tribe

*The undead's habit
of eating its shroud
– see p. 20*

– see p. 20

*This is the
original purpose
of tombstones –
to weigh down
the dead, as
well as to
identify them*

FIGURE 22
THE VAMPIRE SLAYER'S
STAKE AND MALLET. THE
STAKE SHOULD BE OF
SUFFICIENT CALIBRE NOT
ONLY TO CAUSE PHYSICAL
DAMAGE BUT ALSO TO
SYMBOLICALLY PIN THE
REVENANT TO THE EARTH.

103

of East Africa go one step further: should a man hang himself from a tree, it is uprooted and burned to ash; he is cremated and buried at a crossroads, and a pile of stones is erected on the grave.

Binding

Corpse binding is a well-known anti-vampiric. In certain countries, twine and rope are used to tie the toes, feet, knees, legs or entire body of the deceased, thus restricting its movement. Often, the binding is cut prior to burial, leaving a series of knots; should the corpse become a vampire, it will be compelled to untie every knot before proceeding.

A more guaranteed binding comes in the form of thorny lengths of briar – a fetter of rose, hawthorn and whitethorn carefully wound around the legs, body or head provides both a physical and a symbolic binding. Should an evil spirit then force its way into the corpse, not only will the twigs prevent the vampire from rising, but any movement will cause it to be pricked, trapped and possibly even killed by the sharp thorns.

Thorns may also be picked off the twigs and scattered in the coffin. You may even wish to consider sewing or sticking the spines into the winding sheet or burial clothes. Both of these methods have the effect of pinning the corpse symbolically. Similarly, thorns scattered

Throw a ball of tangled string into the coffin to keep the vampire busy

over the sealed grave will prevent any further post-mortem movements.

A tight swaddling can also be wrapped around the corpse. This not only restricts the revenant's movement, but gives it something to chew on, or pick at, once it reanimates.

Finally, the Balkans and Slavs have provided the vampire hunter with another valuable method of binding: wrapping the corpse tightly in a carpet before burial. Combined, perhaps, with some of the other binding methods suggested here, it may not stop the vampire coming into being, but it will at least prevent it from wandering the earth.

In China, iron nails, peas and sometimes rice grains are scattered over the grave to prevent the vampire from surfacing

† Plants and Herbalism

THE VAMPIRE, being a grotesque aberration of nature, holds in contempt all that is pure, holy and natural. Thus, an abundance of plant life exists with powerful anti-vampiric qualities. Garlic and the stake of hawthorn are two enduring examples, although the vampire hunter is advised to acquaint himself with some of the less common flora.

In Scandinavian myth, a giant ash tree called yggdrasil sits at the centre of the world, its roots and branches connecting heaven, hell and earth. Significant?

ASH (*Fraxinus excelsior*): The "tree of life", an evergreen with powerful symbolic connections to purity and goodness, hence its use as a source for vampire-killing stakes throughout northern Europe and Russia. It was the Roman statesman Pliny the Elder (AD 23–79) who identified ash as the natural enemy of evil.

ASPEN (*Populus tremula*): Also known as the trembling or quaking poplar. Its potency against evil stems from its religious significance: it was the wood used to make Christ's cross, hence the belief that the tree now trembles in shame.

BUCKTHORN (*Rhamnus cathartica*): The ancient Greeks were the first to seize upon the sharp thorns of this plant as a protection from the undead. Its thorny branches were hung above doors and windows to ward off evil and prevent wandering spirits returning to their homes. Twigs of buckthorn should be placed inside the coffin of a suspected vampire.

CHRIST'S THORN (*Paliurus spina-christi*): The thorny shrub believed to have formed Christ's crown of thorns. To the vampire, it has the same effect as buckthorn – to which it is related – but, because of its religious significance, it possesses increased potency.

GARLIC (*Allium sativum*): The very symbol of the power of nature against the vampire. A pungent member of the onion family, it has many different uses to the vampire slayer: as a protective, a repellent and a weapon (*see page 118*).

HAWTHORN (*Crataegus monogyna*): Also known as may, quickthorn or whitethorn. Considered unlucky in England if brought into the home, elsewhere in Europe it is an essential tool of the vampire hunter. Hang it on lintels to ward off evil, scatter the thorns in coffins to pin the vampire in place symbolically, and use its lengthy twigs to bind the corpse.

HOLLY (*Ilex aquifolium*): An evergreen shrub hung on doors and windows as a protective since Roman times. A powerful symbol of Christmas, a brooch of holly is recommended when vampire hunting.

Chasing a vampire into a bush of hawthorn will kill it instantly

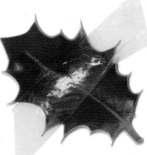

A German vampire watcher once told me to always carry a lemon: stuff it in the mouth of the corpse to prevent it coming back to life. Worth a try!

✝ JUNIPER (*Juniperus communis*): Evergreen shrub that, according to Gypsy lore, will repel evil. The dark berries can also be crushed and the resulting pulp, with its familiar, pungent aroma (recognizable to any drinker of gin), used as a protective unguent.

LIME TREE (*Tilia europaea*): Also known as the linden tree (and not to be confused with the fruit-bearing *Citrus aurantifolia*). Stakes are commonly carved from the branches of this deciduous tree, a native of northern Europe.

MAPLE (*Acer campestre*): A popular source of wood for impaling vampires, particularly in the colder regions of northern Russia and China.

MILLET (*Panicum miliaceum*): A widely grown cereal, millet can be rubbed into the eyes of a corpse and used it to plug orifices to prevent possession by a wandering spirit. It can also be used to distract the walking dead if scattered in its path.

MUSTARD SEED (*Brassica nigra, B. hirta*): It is widely held that vampires have an obsessive nature, and will be compelled to pick up – and often eat – seeds and grains scattered in its path. Mustard seeds have a particular religious significance in certain vampire-rich regions of the Balkans, and are doubly effective.

POPLAR (*Populus*): This majestic tree is a less popular, but no less effective, source of wood for stakes. It is commonly found in northern, temperate climes.

ROSE (*Rosa*): A prickly shrub with powerful scented flowers. A symbol of love, beauty and purity, the first rose is said to have appeared miraculously in Bethlehem. In Transylvania, a flower may be placed on the chest of a corpse to prevent reanimation. The thorns of the rose may also be scattered in the coffin, pricked into the shroud or strewn across a grave to pin the revenant to its final resting place.

Dog rose thorns seem particularly effective

Wear strong cologne — vampires hate perfumed scents

ROWAN (*Sorbus aucuparia*): Venerated by druids for its power to ward off witches, the rowan tree, mountain ash or witch wood can be used to carve stakes and protective amulets.

WILLOW (*Salix*): A mystical tree, the willow is the source of magical power and a good source of stake wood. Initiates of earth-energy deem forked willow branches to be the most sensitive dowsing rods, and the tree's narrow leaves, when stewed or chewed, are a powerful palliative.

WOLFSBANE (*Aconitum lycoctonum*): Poisonous member of the buttercup family, wolfsbane is known to have power over evil. Hang on doors and windows as a protective.

† Offerings and Sacrifices

ᴵT IS COMMONLY BELIEVED that a ravenous vampire can be appeased with offerings, usually in the form of food and drink. This theory is based on the understanding that the dead take on a material form, and may be appeased by particular types of gift.

Leaving food at the side of a grave was a common pagan practice

FIGURE 23

THE JACK-O'-LANTERN: A LIGHTED BEACON GUIDING OUR ANCESTORS BACK HOME. BEWARE, HOWEVER: THE BOSNIAN GYPSY BELIEVE THAT PUMPKINS, TOMATOES AND MELONS CAN SHELTER THE SPIRIT OF A VAMPIRE (THE OFFENDING FRUIT MUST BE BOILED TO EXORCIZE THE UNDEAD).

to ensure that the dead did not rise and seek out their own sustenance. The ceremony of the wake – the feasting that follows a funeral – is another throwback to the superstitious pagan need to share food with the deceased.

Offerings are most effective when made during festivals that celebrate the dead. On such feast days, the veil between this world and the afterlife is at its thinnest, and the dead walk the earth, revisiting friends and family. One such festival was the Greek Anthesteria. During this three-day celebration, the dead would rejoin their families and give thanks for the grapes and the coming spring. Cups would overflow with wine – the festival was associated with Dionysus, the god of fertility and wine – and the dead propitiated with lavish feasts. With the kindly ancestors, however, came the mischievous spirits. So to ward off unwanted visitors, the temples and churches would be symbolically roped off, and bouquets of briar hung on the lintels. At the end the festival, the dead were told: "Out of the house with you, out of doors, ye ghosts. The Anthesteria is over."

Another significant festival is Samhain, the Celtic festival on which Hallowe'en is based. The first day of November is the start of the pagan new year and a time for new beginnings. During the Samhain celebrations, the spirits of our ancestors pay us a visit, guided home by lighted turnips left on the threshold (the origin of our Jack-o'-lanterns). To show our respect for the dead, an extra place should be set at the dining table, and milk and bread offered for sustenance, lest they attempt to find their food by other more horrid means.

"Soul cakes" are another feasting tradition around this time of the year. Simple biscuits, they are intended as nourishment for the dead, and were traditionally baked on All Souls' Day (2nd November). Once baked, the biscuits should be thrown in the fire, handed around friends, family and neighbours, or offered to the poor, who act as deputies for the dead.

Milk can be left out for the dead, or drank to honour the ancestors; the Damaras of Namibia worship their dead by pouring it on to their graves.

Pronounced "sow-en" or "sow-an"

Grandma's Soul Cake recipe:

1. Melt together 100g butter, 50g brown sugar & 2 tbsp treacle
2. Stir in 2 tbsp golden syrup & 175 ml milk
3. Add 100g flour, 2 tsp baking powder, 1/2 tsp each of ground ginger, cinnamon and cloves & stir in 100g oats
4. Bake for 45–60 mins at 180C / 350F

Slaying Vampires

The killing of a vampire – what we call the "Great Reparation" – requires cunning, valour and a mastery of the necessary tools and techniques.

AVING LEARNED to identify, locate and prevent the undead from walking the earth, it is critical that you now understand how to kill these wicked pests. For, when all else fails – when absolution, or a scattering of seeds, or a binding of briar does not curb the diabolical urges – it is time for the Great Reparation: the slaying, once and for all, of the vampire.

Up to this point, we have been investigating methods aimed at preventing the vampire from coming into being or trying to restrict its post-mortem movements. The purpose of the Great Reparation, however, is the dissolution of the body of the vampire followed by the release of the spirit lodged or trapped therein. This necessitates combining the knowledge gained so far – of plants, distracting knots, symbolic bindings, and so on – with an understanding of the tools and techniques for killing what is already dead.

Over the coming pages, I will outline the various items of equipment that the prepared vampire slayer must consider carrying during a hunt. These include objects and amulets that repel a bloodthirsty revenant, as well as those that will help you to kill him. I will also provide you with basic guidelines for protective and expulsive magic, and advice on dealing with the undead if you are unfortunate enough to be unarmed.

I must stress that the staking and/or burning of a body should only ever be performed when you are absolutely sure of the existence of the vampire. Certainty that bindings, restrictions and absolutions have all failed are necessary before you decide to hack up a corpse or reduce it to ash.

STAKES FOR HIRE

At this juncture, it is worth mentioning the historical role of itinerant vampire slayers. These mercenary hunters travel from village to village trading on their professed skills in dispatching the undead. The *vampirdzhija* and *djadadjii* of Bulgaria, for example, claim to be able to sense a revenant before it is formed, and will take measures to rid a town of its "infestation" – for a substantial fee, no doubt. Similarly, the *maw du* of the Philippines, the Serbian Gypsy *dhampirs*, the Sabbatarians of Greece and even Catholic clerics have been known to hire themselves out as vampire hunters.

Needless to say, you should always be wary of such self-professed slayers: many of the vampire "epidemics" reported in the eighteenth century were undoubtedly the results of charlatans – and clerics – cashing in on paranoia and hysteria. Instead, entrust the more ecclesiastical aspects of vampire slaying, such as the anointing of equipment or holy water, to a dependable priest who understands the history and folklore of the vampire; the assistance of a trusted psychic or white witch is also to be advised.

† The Vampire Hunter's Kit

THERE ARE NO universal rules for slaying vampires. Accepted beliefs as to the efficacy of weapons such as the wooden stake or crucifix change from era to era and country to country. Indeed, the effect on vampires of even the ubiquitous garlic clove differs as you cross the continents.

Instead, the modern vampire hunter is advised to familiarize himself with a wide range of vampire myths and legends. Folklore, oral traditions and even fictional literature may offer a rich heritage from which slayers can learn their dark art – and study the essential anti-vampire tools.

The slayer's greatest ally – after intelligence and cunning, of course – is therefore a well-stocked kitbag. The following inventory lists what this author considers the minimum of kit for tackling a physical vampire.

GARLIC: A braid of fresh garlic keeps longer than individual bulbs, and can be worn around the neck or hung on doors. See FIGURE 26.

STAKES: A two-foot-long stake of sharpened wood (preferably hawthorn) is essential for

FIGURE 24 *A slayer's basic arsenal*
GARLIC, WOODEN STAKE, CRUCIFIX, HOLY WATER,
MIRROR, SUNFLOWER SEEDS

115

Also useful are:

- *Torch and portable ultraviolet light*
- *Multi-function penknife*
- *Hacksaw with spare new blades*
- *Canister of fuel*
- *Wind-proof lighter (or matches)*
- *Map of the area*

FIGURE 25

ENGRAVING, C. SIXTEENTH CENTURY, REPRODUCED IN *Les Tribunaux Secrets* (1864). A BOHEMIAN VAMPIRE IS SLAIN WITH THE EXPLOSIVE THRUST OF A RED-HOT IRON THROUGH THE CHEST.

pinning or killing a sleeping or buried vampire; a quiver of smaller stakes is suggested for close combat. See FIGURE 27.

CRUCIFIX: A vampire repellent: can be used to inflict physical damage by pressing it against their flesh (proximity is not recommended). See FIGURE 28.

MIRROR: A useful tool for identifying the undead, as they cast no reflection. Some vampires are also repelled by mirrors as they cannot cope with this lack of reflection. Can also be used to reflect beams of sunlight on to a vampire. See FIGURE 29.

HOLY WATER: Secure yourself a phial or bottle of holy water, another vampire repellent. Scatter on unholy ground to detect revenants, throw in the face as a weapon, or use as an anointer for protection. See FIGURE 30.

SEEDS AND KNOTS: Scattered seeds have been known to distract vampires, who in certain regions will be compelled to pick up every last one; useful if being pursued by a revenant.

OTHER TOOLS: Additional equipment with which the slayer should become acquainted include a mallet, chisel, axe, sack, rope, blades, spade, crowbar and pincers. See FIGURE 31.

† Garlic

O F THE ENTIRE FLORA known to vampire hunters, garlic (*Allium sativum*) is the most potent and intoxicating. The Arabs believe that garlic first sprung from the left footprint of Satan as he stepped from the Garden of Eden, and the ancient Greek priestesses banned from their temples anyone with the smell of garlic on their breath. Even today, the Jains number garlic among the foods that should not be eaten, and those practising Sadhanas outlaw garlic as it is thought to impair the mind. However, garlic is well known today as an antibiotic and antiseptic, and it afforded our ancestors untold strength – both mental and physical – against any ills or foes.

FIGURE 26

GARLIC (*Allium sativum*), A MEMBER OF THE ONION FAMILY. IT HAS BEEN CULTIVATED AS A CURATIVE AND HERB SINCE ANTIQUITY. AS A DEFENCE AGAINST VAMPIRES, IT IS MOST EFFECTIVE WHEN THE CLOVES ARE CRUSHED.

Egyptian papyri dating from around 1500 BC prescribe at least twenty-two garlic remedies for a range of ailments including headache and fatigue, and the builders of the great pyramids were energized by the beneficial bulbs. Similarly, the Roman legions went to battle emboldened by a meal of garlic cloves. Its salutary effects were also known to eighteenth-century graverobbers, who would bathe in garlic-infused vinegars to immunize themselves against the plague.

Garlic's power as a charm against vampires, however, lies in its potent odour. The theory is that like repels like, so a foul-smelling vampire will naturally be repelled by anything equally odiferous. This accounts for the use of incense during religious occasions, and why any strong-smelling substance – from sulphur to excrement – can be smeared around doorways to prevent a vampire from passing.

Braids of garlic (*see page 71*) were – and, indeed, still are – worn around the neck by many Eastern European peoples, and crushed garlic is used to anoint everything from newborn babies and cattle to the entrances and windows of homes and churches.

Similarly, to prevent the spirit of a vampire from taking over a corpse, the orifices should be stuffed with garlic and cloves scattered inside the coffin. A slain vampire should also have garlic stuffed into its mouth; if decapitated, a bulb must be placed between the head and the neck.

Garlic can also be used to detect vampires. In Slavic countries, anyone who refuses to eat garlic risks being staked – in the past, church congregations were expected to show their faith by consuming raw garlic before the service began. Thus, the vampire hunter is advised to prepare a phial of garlic oil to be carried at all times – it can be used as both a weapon and a means of detection.

Crush 2 cloves of garlic and add to 50ml vegetable oil. Keep in a sealed bottle.

Rub a crushed clove on your neck to prevent a vampire from biting

† Stakes

URING VAMPIRE EPIDEMICS, especially in Eastern Europe and the Balkans, efforts were taken to ensure that buried corpses would not return to life. Traditionally, a sharpened stake was thrust through the corpse's stomach, pinning it to the earth. Similarly, nails and pins were inserted into the body, symbolically fixing the corpse to the soil. Should an evil spirit then attempt to possess the corpse, it would be unable to escape from its grave.

Sharpened stakes were also pushed into the ground above the graves of potential vampires. Any revenant attempting to claw its way to surface would then be impaled and either killed or pinned indefinitely to the earth.

The wooden stake – ash, aspen, willow, hawthorn and juniper are popular choices – has since been adopted as a weapon in the fight against vampires. Some cultures believe that the vampire's heart continues to beat and that hammering a stake through it releases the spirit and brings a final end to the physical body. In some cultures, it is considered vital that the deed be done in one continuous action, lest the vampire fights back and kills its attacker.

It is imperative, therefore, that the modern vampire hunter has at his disposal a

FIGURE 27
HAND-MADE STAKES:
EXAMPLES SHOWN ARE
FASHIONED FROM A
FALLEN BRANCH OF ASH.
REMOVE THE SIDE SHOOTS
AND USE A SHARP KNIFE
TO CARVE AWAY FROM
YOURSELF TO SHAPE
THE POINT.

ready supply of sharpened stakes. A variety of sizes is also strongly recommended: longer, thicker stakes for pinning (a mallet is also likely to be required), and smaller, lighter stakes for combat.

In Russia, I am told, a vampire can only be killed with one thrust of the stake. Stab again and it comes back to life.

† Crucifix

AS WE ALREADY KNOW, the religious symbol or icon is a powerful ally in the fight against the servants of Satan. And against the vampire there is no more potent a device than the crucifix – representing the cross that bore the crucified body of Christ.

Alone, the cross is invaluable as an anti-vampiric; not only is it the most ancient and universal of all symbols, but, unlike other religious imagery, it can be quickly improvised with anything from stakes and swords to sticks and fingers. It can even be drawn in the air or across the chest to provide the vampire hunter with instant divine protection.

A cross of tar or resin painted on the lid of a coffin – or on the door of a house or barn – prevents the undead from passing. Similarly, a wax seal in the shape of an "X" is the preferred choice for physically and symbolically closing the lips of the deceased: with the mouth thus protected, no evil will be able to enter the corpse and take possession.

As a powerful mystical shape, the cross plays a role in a number of magical rites for protection and banishment. In many cultures throughout the world, crossroads even have a supernatural significance as the recommended burial site for witches and vampires (both

† Latin † Greek ☦ Russian

preferably having been "earthed" with a wooden stake through the chest or heart).

However, the crucifix, the emblem of Christ's martyrdom and suffering, comes ready charged with powerful religious energy. If you wear a crucifix on a sturdy chain around the neck for protection, the very sight of it will repel a vampire. The slayer's kit should contain at least one larger crucifix, as such "weapons" will not only repel the undead but cause actual physical pain when pressed into their pale skin. Furthermore, a crucifix left in a grave will render it uninhabitable to vampires; one buried with the deceased should prevent the vampire coming into being.

FIGURE 28

THE CRUCIFIX FIRST APPEARED AS A RELIGIOUS ICON IN THE FIFTH CENTURY BC, AND HAS PROVED A MOST VALUABLE WEAPON AGAINST EVIL. THE CROSS IS NOT SOLELY A CHRISTIAN EMBLEM – IT IS, ARGUABLY, THE OLDEST AND MOST UNIVERSAL OF SYMBOLS.

The effect of the crucifix can be augmented by being blessed by a priest and anointed with holy water. When wielding the crucifix against the undead, you may discover that your faith in its spiritual potency redoubles its power. As you present the crucifix, chant: "O vampire, look upon this. Here is Jesus Christ who loosed us from the pains of Hell and died for us upon the tree!"

 Constantine

 Celtic

† Mirror

IT WAS ONCE BELIEVED that the Devil created the mirror in order to trap wandering souls. Indeed, there are many superstitions and fables associated with reflective surfaces, from still water to polished stones. In hospitals, the poorly are encouraged to avoid looking at their reflection, and mirrors are traditionally covered up or turned against the wall after a death.

Some claim that it is even unlucky to sleep near a mirror. Why? Because it is feared that the soul, projecting out of the body, will become trapped behind the glass, never to return. This is one reason why it is considered * bad luck to break a mirror: a soul caught in the looking glass could never return if it were smashed. Another reason is that mirrors were once believed to hold visions of the future, and that a shattered mirror symbolized no future.

In the Andaman Islands, a still pool of water is considered to reflect not your face but your soul. The Zulu believe that by staring into a dark pool of water, you risk your soul being devoured by a supernatural beast.

FIGURE 29

THE VAMPIRE'S LACK OF REFLECTION MAY BE MORE OF A FICTIONAL CONCEIT THAN A REALITY, BUT THE WELL-PREPARED SLAYER SHOULD NEVERTHELESS ALWAYS CARRY A HANDHELD MIRROR. NOTHING SHOULD BE LEFT TO CHANCE.

* Burying the broken pieces is believed to reverse the bad luck

And the people of (Basutoland) dread crossing a stream for fear of losing their soul to a passing crocodile.

Known since 1966 as Lesotho

So how does this relate to the hunting of vampires? Once again, Bram Stoker has much to answer for, as it was he who conceived the idea of the vampire having no reflection. Jonathan Harker witnesses Dracula hurling his shaving mirror out of window, the vicious Count angered by his lack of reflection, a cruel reminder of his abhorrent, undead state.

While this may be fiction, there are some historical precedents. The Chinese believe that mirrors can repel evil forces, and during the religious ceremonies of the Ibo and Kalabari of Nigeria, evil spirits seeking to attack the souls of men are tricked into fighting the "soul" reflected in glass.

The same reason why cultures such as the Inuit feared having their photographs taken – in case the camera stole the soul

It is worth carrying a small vanity mirror to aid in the hunt for vampires and evil spirits. If a body casts no reflection, assume it is one of the undead and take appropriate measures. However, the suspected vampire may still reflect, so remain cautious. Mirrors can also be used to detect signs of life in vampires or their victims: hold the glass over the lips and look for condensation.

The handheld mirror may also be used to reflect a beam of sunlight on to a vampire or suspected corpse. On contact with the sun, the skin of the vampire is liable to boil and blister.

Beware that sunlight only appears to harm certain species of vampire. In parts of Greece, Russia and Poland, the undead may walk the streets at any time of the day.

125

† Holy Water

WATER, THE UNIVERSAL SOLVENT, is the oldest symbol of purification and cleansing. It follows, then, that water blessed by a priest – holy water – should have added potency as a weapon against evil.

Like the crucifix, holy water appears to have been introduced at some time around the fourth century. However, water – and in particular, fast-flowing water – has always been used to flush away wickedness and evil. As discussed previously,

FIGURE 30

A SIMPLE PHIAL OF HOLY WATER WILL HELP YOU NOT ONLY TO LOCATE VAMPIRES BUT ALSO TO DESTROY THEM. AND IN THE PROPER HANDS, EVEN AN EMPTY VESSEL CAN PROVE ANTI-VAMPIRIC.

vampires are unable to cross fast-flowing or salt water, which is why the Greeks would disinter suspected revenants and bury them on remote, uninhabited islands. The decapitated heads, dismembered limbs or eviscerated organs of vampires are often tossed into rivers, as are sackfuls of ashes following vampire cremations. In the infamous *Malleus Maleficarum*, the witch finder's handbook, instructions are given for the *iudicium aqua*, or "trial by water". Throw a suspected witch in a river: if she floats, she is a witch; if she drowns, she is innocent.

Holy water, however, provides the vampire hunter with a portable – and potable – form of protection and attack, so you should always keep a ready supply. Clerics usually sprinkle holy water from a dispenser known as an aspergillum, but the inventive vampire hunter will use any means possible of collecting and transporting the precious fluid.

Ask a friendly priest to anoint bottles of water, or fill your canteen from his fount. Alternatively, if you have faith, bless the water (and oil, if you wish holy oil) yourself:

> "We bless this water in the Name of Jesus Christ, Thy only Son; we invoke upon this water and this oil the Name of Him Who suffered, Who was crucified, Who arose from the dead, and Who sits at the right of the Uncreated. Grant unto these creatures the power to heal; may all fevers, every evil spirit, and all maladies be put to flight by him who either drinks these beverages or is anointed with them, and may they be a remedy in the Name of Jesus Christ, Thy only Son."

Thus anointed, the water can now be thrown in the face of a vampire, where it will

Buy bottles of mineral water regularly, and have them blessed by the local priest

Or – if a willing priest can't be found, secretly fill the bottles from the holy water stoup near the door of a church

Fill a water pistol with holy water – you might look stupid, but your aim will be perfect!

have the effect of burning like acid. For added protection, you should carry with you at all times an atomizer of holy water; should you suspect danger from any abhorrent demon, you will be able to surround yourself in a fine protective mist.

Blessed water can also be used to detect evil: if you suspect someone of being undead, request that he partake of a sip or two. Or sprinkle it on the ground above suspicious graves – if the soil bubbles and boils, assume a vampire lies beneath.

Finally, I have it on good authority that holy water is a powerful curative. Immerse any wound inflicted during a vampire attack in holy water to reverse any evil side effects.

Bottling a Vampire

Should your phial or canteen of holy water run dry at a crucial moment, have no fear. In the right hands, the empty vessel can be equally as powerful a weapon against the vampire as a sharpened stake.

To explain how this is possible, recall in your mind the story of the fisherman and the jinn. To stave off her impending execution, Scheherazade regales her husband Sultan Schahriah with a thousand-and-one nights of wonderful tales, starting with that of a poor fisherman who finds a brass bottle. When the hapless man unstops the lead bung, a mist

jinn =
a genie

pours out and condenses into the form of a *jinn* ✝
– one of the demons of Arabian mythology. For
eighteen-hundred years the demon has been
trapped inside, and yet, by the end of the tale,
the wily fisherman has tricked the demon back
into the bottle.

Like the *jinn*, vampires can be bottled. First
you must force the revenant into a corner using
a crucifix, icon or any other powerful vampire
repellent. Have the opened bottle at the ready,
preferably primed with a piece of food or – in
the absence of anything else – your own blood.
Faced with the crucifix or icon, the vampire will
have nowhere to run, except into the bottle, at
which point you quickly plug it with a cork.

In Bulgaria, the infamous *vampirdzhija* –
the mercenary sorcerers who perform this
dangerous function (*see page 113*) – complete
their task by tossing the bottle into a roaring
fire; in Malaya, the receptacle – a bamboo
tabong sealed with leaves and a magical charm
– is thrown into the sea.

† Seeds and Knots

IT MAY COME as a surprise to some that a vampire can be rendered powerless with the simple scattering of a handful of seeds. For this is one aspect of the supernatural which is rarely alluded to in the vulgar melodramas.

Seeds are charged not only with the germ of a new life, but also with power over the undead. A sprinkling of, say, carrot seed will completely wrong-foot the vampire, who will be compelled to delay his diabolical mission until every last seed has been picked up or eaten. Unfortunately for the revenant, it may take a year to swallow each pellet, giving the vampire slayer ample opportunity to administer their rough justice.

Is it the life-affirming symbolism of the seed that so distracts the vampire? Arguably so, as we know that the fiend loathes all that is pure and natural. However, the undead are obsessed not just with seed: millet, pebbles, rice and even iron filings may all have the same distracting effect. Mustard seed (*Brassica nigra*, *B. hirta*) is widely considered to be the most effective, perhaps owing to its medicinal and healing properties, or indeed to its role in Christ's parable, "The Kingdom of Heaven is like a mustard seed …" (Matthew 13, *31*). Poppy seeds are also known to be very effective, their

In Romania, salt is a very important anti-vampiric – pregnant women eat it raw to prevent giving birth to a vampire (not very good for you otherwise!)

Use salt to draw a cross on top of a suspect coffin

narcotic properties no doubt helping to soothe the savage beast, as are linseeds from flax (*Linum usitatissimum*).

In addition to those mentioned above, you should also consider scattering combinations of sea salt, sea sand, oats, peppercorns, corn kernels, peas and iron nails (which also have a powerful "pinning" symbolism).

A good supply of pellets of one form or another has many uses. Place some in the mouth of a suspected vampire, scatter more over the body, or pour them into the coffin. Consider also mixing them into the backfill after a burial – should the revenant claw its up way up through the soil, it will become engrossed in picking out the seeds.

Scatter more seeds on top of the grave, or around the perimeter of the cemetery. Throw them into barns to protect cattle, across the threshold to bar the revenant entry, or wear them in a protective amulet. Most effective is a trail of grains leading into a thicket of thorny shrubs, where the vampire will hopefully become trapped.

Finally, if you can, take your lead from the vampire hunters of Surinam. To distract the bloodsucking *asema*, they scatter rice grains mixed with nail clippings from the talons of an owl. If the *asema* picks up a nail, it is pricked, whereupon it drops the seeds already collected and has to start again.

Instead of seeds, could try

- Dried peas / beans
- Ball-bearings
- Peanuts
- Crumbled seed bars
- Cornflakes

And if a family is being terrorized by a vampire, lay a trail of seeds from their home to the nearest cemetery – or to right inside the burning chamber of a crematorium!

✝ *Knots*

The vampire of Europe – and particularly Germany – has a strange, obsessive compulsion to unpick knots. When faced with a tangled length of string, the vampire will be unable to proceed until every knot is untied, a task that may take the creature one year for every knot.

Knots have a great mystical significance, particularly to witches, who use them in the casting of spells. Objects and emotions can be magically entwined or ensnared in the loops of a ligature, and in some cultures it is even believed that a knot can trap a soul. Endless knots such as the Celtic knot – and indeed the pentagram – are symbols of continuity, longevity and eternity; Tibetan Buddhist art is often embellished with the "glorious interwoven knot of life", signifying the never-ending teachings of Buddha.

The aim of the vampire slayer, then, is to tie the equivalent of the Gordian knot. This can be achieved by placing a tangled ball of wool, string or thread in the coffin of a suspected revenant, or binding the body with netting. To occupy the meticulous vampire, the Greeks place fishnets in the grave, while the Gypsies hang nets, often interwoven with garlic bulbs, over their doors and windows. I have even heard that a common kitchen sieve hung on a door is distracting: the revenant will be driven to count each hole.

Finally, as with the seeds, use thread to lure the vampire to its death. String a knotted cord from the creature's grave to – and through – a thorny thicket; when the vampire reaches into the bush to untie yet another knot, he will become trapped, pricked and hopefully killed.

In the 4th century BC, Gordius, King of Gordium (located in modern-day Turkey), tied a knot so intricate that none could untie it. "Whoever undid the knot would reign over the whole East," he prophesied. Alexander the Great rose to the challenge by slicing the knot with his sword.

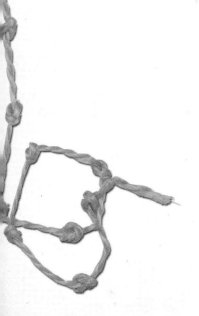

† Other Tools

IN ADDITION TO the aforementioned vampire-slaying arsenal, the well-prepared hunter must also ensure ready access to a range of ancillary implements. Such additions to the slayer's kit fall into one of two main forms – tool or weapon – although it should be noted that the two are not mutually exclusive.

AXE: The vampire slayer will find many uses for such a tool. A felling or woodman's axe is strongly recommended for hewing down wood for stakes; a smaller kitchen hatchet is more suitable for shaping the wood.

Portability should be considered, as it is beneficial to have a hatchet of some sort in your kitbag (or strapped across the back). Use it for cleaving apart chains, gaining access to crypts, and, of course, decapitating or dismembering the undead. I advise that you get accustomed to using the axe in combat, should the need arise. If you find yourself in a churchyard and in need of an axe, call in on the sexton. He should be able to provide a number of useful tools.

SPADE: Another tool that may be borrowed from a sexton, the spade is not just for digging holes. If not too blunt, the blade can be useful for decapitating a sleeping revenant; use the flat

Other useful tools / weapons:

- *Crossbow*
- *Bolt gun*
- *Saw*
- *Holy relic or Icon (painting of Christ or the Madonna)*

FIGURE 31 *Useful ancillary slaying tools*
AXE, SPADE, CROWBAR, SICKLE, ROPE OR TWINE, SACK

side for pounding a stake through their chest. With the handle of an axe or other suitably long implement, the shaft of the spade can also be wielded as a repellent, makeshift cross.

MALLET: The weapon of choice for Thor – the Norse God of War – the mallet is a symbol of power over evil. In addition to its use together with a chisel in sharpening stakes, it can be used by the slayer to strike a sharpened length into the chest of the vampire, particularly in regions where a single blow is required. The mallet is also useful for breaking the bones and generally crippling a corpse that has been cursed by vampirism.

BLADES: A dagger or sword is a valuable weapon against the undead, particularly if blessed by a priest. Use in the same way as a stake, and remember that a pair can also be crossed. Use also to excise the heart or cut the hamstrings of a sleeping revenant.

CROWBAR: To provide leverage when attempting to gain entry to sealed tombs, crypts and coffins. Can also be used to good effect as a bone-breaker.

PINCERS: Use the jaws of this tool to extract nails from coffins, or teeth from mouths. Nails drawn from the coffin of a suspected vampire

can be crafted into protective amulets or, as practised in China, mixed with peas and rice and scattered over the grave to pin the beast to its final resting place.

ROPE: A good length of tough rope will serve many purposes: binding a corpse, dragging a coffin from the earth, and – when knotted – distracting a vampire. A sorcerer or witch may also offer to use the rope in spell casting or as part of a magical rite.

SICKLE: Throughout Eastern Europe and the Balkans, it is considered wise to bury a suspect vampire with a sickle. Place it in the coffin or lay it across the neck of the corpse – when the vampire stirs, it will be pricked or decapitated. A sickle is also a useful tool for combating overgrown cemeteries.

SACK: A useful all-purpose sack will serve you well for collecting bones, ashes and body parts that may need to be flung into a flowing river. Be sure that the sack can be securely fastened with rope. Alternatively, the sack can be slipped over the upper body of a revenant to restrict movement, affording you extra time to ready your attack.

† Unarmed Combat

THERE WILL BE TIMES when, no matter how well prepared, the vampire slayer will encounter his ungodly foe without weapons or protection. In such unenviable circumstances, it is vital to exploit some basic self-defence techniques. I am indebted, therefore, to my good friend Michael Flynn, an initiate of the martial arts, for the advice that follows.

Parry and Punch

Should a vampire reach out to grab your throat, sweep his arm away to the right with the flat palm of your left hand, moving from the hip as if pushing against a door. As the hand of the beast passes harmlessly by your right shoulder, step in with your right foot, throw your weight forward from the right hip and deliver a hard, low punch to the floating rib.

This is at the base of the rib cage and is the easiest to break

Nerve Strike

Use this move if the revenant has both hands clasped around your neck. Jam both of your arms up into the space between the vampire's arms and place the index finger of each hand into the hollows behind the creature's ears where the jawbone joins the skull. Using his arm for leverage, push your index fingers inward and upward into these hollows with all the strength you can muster. As soon as you feel the grip loosen (and it will), bend forward from the hips and pull his head toward you, striking his nose with your forehead before pulling him down to the ground. Now run.

"Number 4" Block

If a vampire attacks from your right-hand side, block his strike with the outside edge of your left forearm (that way you will not expose any major veins or arteries). Hook your right arm behind the creature's upper right arm and thread it through until your right hand is able to grip your left wrist, forming the shape of the number "4". Lifting slightly, step forward quickly and listen out for the "pop" as the creature's arm and shoulder socket part company. Keep pulling until the arm comes away in your hand.

– then beat the vampire unconscious with the soggy end!!

Neck Snap

This move is suitable if you have wrestled the vampire into a prone position on the ground. From this position, snapping a neck is a little like unscrewing a tight-fitting lid from a jar. Kneel on the vermin's back and wrap your right arm round his neck to the point where you can reach all the way around his head and cradle his chin in the crook of your elbow. With your left hand, grip the vampire's forehead and rotate his entire head clockwise at speed. Continue to turn until you hear his neck snap.

† Armed Combat

Parry and Stab

An adaptation of the "parry and punch" manoeuvre (*see page 138*), this technique uses a wooden stake as an extension of the arm.

As your attacker reaches out to grab your throat, sweep the arm away to the right with the flat palm of your left hand, moving from the hip as if pushing against a door. Step in with your right foot, throw your weight forward from the right hip and, while the whole of one side of the creature's body is exposed, strike hard at the centre of the rib cage, driving the stake through to the heart and killing the beast.

Jo strike

This attack makes use of a *jo*, a long, blunt pole. (A wooden stick or length of scaffolding may also suffice.)

Hold the pole out in front of you and grip as if you were holding a rope, your hands about a foot apart. Bring the pole up until it almost touches your back. Now bring the pole back down by describing a circle with your hands, pushing the right hand forward over the left. As you do this, step forward with the right foot and move your weight on to your right hip so that the full force of your body is behind the pole as it comes down on to the revenant's skull.

As used in the martial art aikido

Bottle

It is sometimes necessary to improvise a weapon from whatever lies at hand. Should a bottle be available, consider yourself fortunate. Do not waste time smashing it against a hard surface. Instead, in the manner of a backhand stroke in the game of tennis, hit the vampire in the face with the bottle, smashing it above the top lip and directly below the nose. On the return swing, jam the now broken bottle into the vampire's chest.

The Two-handed Sword

When all else fails, the two-handed sword can be relied upon to solve most problems.*

Known to vampire slayers as "The Tonic", the two-handed sword should be held out in front of you using a shortened version of the pole grip. Let the tip drop to the right before swinging the blade downward, to the side and behind you in a smooth arc. Bring the sword back around over your head and strike while stepping forward. Repeat the previous steps, but this time let the sword dip and swing to the left, again advancing by a single step on the downward swing. Keep the swings moving continuously, switching left and right with each strike. This "windmill" action can clear an entire room of vampires while at the same time providing you with the kind of protection that no amount of holy water can supply.

– on the grounds that it cures all evils!

* _Especially if anointed by a priest_

141

Vampire Strongholds

By now you will appreciate that there are many dark and fetid corners of the world that harbour vampires. Previous chapters identified some general habitats and other more specific locations. In closing this book, I will now share with you a selection of what I consider to be key strongholds of vampiric activity.

WHAT FOLLOWS is not a field guide to hunting down our vicious foes. It makes no attempt to reveal the whereabouts of these evil fiends. Instead, it deigns to celebrate vampirism, to identify those places that I feel most symbolize and encapsulate all that vampires and vampire hunting represent. For the successful vampire watcher is nothing if not open minded and willing to immerse himself in vampire culture.

Of course, should you wish to continue your investigations in such areas, it will help if you study regional variations in vampire habitat and behaviour. Immerse yourself in the local folklore and learn the *modi operandi* of the indigenous revenants. Try to gain access to university and museum libraries: you may have to seek permission or pay a membership fee, but the amount of knowledge you can gain will be invaluable.

If you do visit any of the world's renowned vampire centres, first make sure you are well read when it comes to the customs of the local people – and the particular nature of their vampire problem. Spend time talking to people in markets and taverns, inquiring about the legends and superstitions of the area. Most people will be happy to show off their local knowledge if you ask the right questions, and this is a very useful way to discover inside information. Identify key locations of potential vampire activity – the houses, cemeteries and woodland – and devote time to watching human and animal activity throughout the day. Be discreet – and be prepared. Take detailed notes of any unusual or recurring behaviour.

Do not be disappointed if your travels fail to yield direct evidence of vampire activity. The knowledge you can gain about the habitat and origins of different vampire species from around the world can only serve to educate and prepare you for future confrontations.

† Highgate Cemetery

FIGURE 32

HIGHGATE CEMETERY,
LONDON, OPENED 1839.
THIS "VICTORIAN VALHALLA"
(IS) LONDON'S MOST
FASHIONABLE GRAVEYARD.

*Was! Now overgrown
and dilapidated.
Grade II listed.*

THE SPRAWLING, picturesque land-scaped gardens of Highgate Cemetery in North London have been described as the most magical place in the capital. It was built in 1839 (and further extended in 1854) as a solution to critical overcrowding in the cemeteries of Central London, a result of the poverty and cholera epidemics of the time.

Burial sites of the nineteenth century were generally inadequate and unsanitary, with grave robbing and body snatching rife. Highgate offered an alternative to this rot and decay: death was treated with reverence and respect, and the wealthier citizens of Queen Victoria's London were prepared to pay large sums of money to build lavish, ornate tombs and catacombs for friends and family.

Despite its early reputation as a fashionable burial site, Highgate Cemetery rapidly began to deteriorate. Its beautifully designed gardens became wild and unmanageable, with dense undergrowth covering many of the gravestones and memorials. The once-proud mausoleums (many reaching three storeys in height and forming what the so-called "Avenues of Death") and catacombs were vandalized, desecrated and exposed to the elements. Once people became afraid of the urban wilderness and its violated tombs, Highgate Cemetery quickly developed sinister associations.*

This gothic burial site has seen a great deal of activity from beyond the grave. Most dramatically, caskets containing the recently deceased were reported to have exploded in Highgate's extensive catacombs. Burial rules at the time stated that coffins had to be encased in lead: with space for up to 850 bodies in the catacombs, this resulted in a dangerous build-up of gases as the corpses decayed inside their caskets. In extreme cases coffins burst open, spewing their rotten contents.

Finally, vampire slayers will perhaps already know Highgate Cemetery as another possible source of inspiration for Bram Stoker's *Dracula*. In the original novel, it is believed to have been the final resting place for Lucy. Her subterranean burial chamber is described as a "death-house in a lonely churchyard, away from teeming London; where … the sun rises over Hampstead Hill".

The cemetery is now famous as the home of the Highgate Vampire:

1967 – Occultist and vampire hunter Sean Manchester investigated sightings of bodies floating out of their graves, and proclaimed that a vampire was active in the area

1970 – 100 people took part in vampire hunt, led by vampirologist David Farrant (who was arrested as a result)

1974 – Manchester believes that he has finally killed the vampire

* The original part of the cemetery was closed in 1975 and underwent extensive conservation work during the following decade

145

† New Orleans

THE HOT AND SULTRY CITY of New Orleans in the state of Louisiana, USA, provides the visitor with a rich mixture of widely differing cultures and beliefs. It has a particularly strong history of voodoo and hoodoo (a type of handed-down voodoo peculiar to New Orleans), as well as long-standing reputation as a rendezvous for ghosts and spirits. It is also an excellent place for vampire watchers and slayers to congregate.

The city has strong nineteenth-century European influences mixed with African and Caribbean folklore and religious tradition, so it should be of no surprise that the vampire has flourished in this part of the world. A particularly good location to begin any search for vampiric or supernatural activity is in the Lafayette Cemetery Number One, which is located in the Garden District and bounded by Washington Avenue, Prytania, Chestnut and Sixth Streets.

FIGURE 33
VOODOO DOLL, NEW ORLEANS, USA. THE DEATH'S-HEAD FIGURINE CAN AFFORD THE VAMPIRE HUNTER GOOD LUCK AND SPIRITUAL PROTECTION IF PROPERLY EMPOWERED BY A WITCH DOCTOR.

This centuries-old "overground" burial site has become known as the "City of the Dead". Residents buried their dead above ground because of the unusually high amount of water in the soil which made traditional forms of burial all but impossible (coffins would literally burst out of the ground on wet and stormy nights). With its ornamental and sometimes beautiful tombs and chambers, the spooky atmosphere of the cemetery attracts many different creatures of the night.

Small shops selling spells and curios used in voodoo ceremonies can be found in the French Quarter of the city, especially around Bourbon Street. These are good places to browse and people-watch, and if this area of the supernatural is of interest you can make enquiries with the proprietor. They may be able to give you information on events or characters in the area.

Other great American garden cemeteries:

– Bellafontaine, St Louis
– Graceland, Chicago
– Mount Auburn, Massachusetts

Things to do:

Visit home of Anne Rice (Vampire Chronicles) – Violin House, 2524 St Charles Avenue (Mon 3–6pm)

Take Haunted History Tour: 2–8 pm, Rev Zombie's Voodoo Shop, 723 St Peter Street

or

Journey Into Darkness: A Vampire Tour – any night, 8:30 pm, front of the St Louis Cathedral

Also Visit 1140 Royal Street (most haunted site in town, apparently!!!)

† Santorini

*T*HERE IS SOMETHING UNIQUE about the ashy black soil of the Cyclades islands of Santorini (the best known of which is Thera). This outcrop in the Aegean Sea is the remains of a dormant volcano, and the fertile earth is rich in volcanic ash but prone to drought. It is rumoured to have antiseptic qualities, and bodies buried in it decay at a very slow rate.

The preserved condition of exhumed corpses naturally led the islanders to believe they had been infested with vampires – and particularly a species known as the *vrykolatios* – and they quickly established themselves as the authority on disposing of the undead. Their reputation was so good, in fact, that Greeks from the mainland delivered corpses suspected of being vampires for disposal, making Santorini the vampire capital of the world.

The islands themselves are beautiful and rugged, clearly showing their violent history of volcanic eruptions. The lowland is made up of hills and long, dark sandy beaches, and there are steep black and red banded cliffs 1,000 feet high as you approach the caldera. When the wind blows in the right direction, the smell of sulphur is carried on the air, providing the startling, sometimes lunar landscape the scent of the underworld.

Because vampires cannot cross running or salt water, they were dumped on islands

Caldera = cauldron (collapsed volcano)

The *Handbook for Travellers in Greece*, published in 1900, details vampire activity in Santorini. The village of Oia at the northern tip, for example, is famous not only for its spectacular sunsets but also for its vampire activity. And many of the towns and villages dotting the islands have reported significant haunting and poltergeist activity.

Finally, students of the fantastical will be eager to investigate the powerful belief of the islanders that the legendary city of Atlantis was located within the islands of Santorini. This grand – and possibly mythical – kingdom was, according to Plato, destroyed by a cataclysmic eruption that sent it to the bottom of the sea. Santorini itself was destroyed by a large volcanic eruption in 1650 BC. We do not know if there is a connection.

Things to do:

- *Check out Thira (Fira) – capital city*
- *Try to find guided vampire tours*
- *Buy some garlic*

FIGURE 34

THE VILLAGE OF OIA – BUILT INTO THE SIDE OF THE CALDERA THAT FORMED WHEN THE ISLAND COLLAPSED IN THE GREAT ERUPTION OF 1650 BC – HAS BEEN NOTED FOR ITS HIGH LEVELS OF VAMPIRIC ACTIVITY.

† Transylvania, Romania

ONE SIGNIFICANT LEGACY of the literature of Bram Stoker is that Transylvania is considered – and not without due cause – to be the home of the vampire. Along with Wallachia, it does indeed have a long and rich history of vampirism, and is today the focus for vampire hunters from around the world.

The author – who never, in fact, travelled to this rugged part of the world – had originally set the first three chapters of *Dracula* in Styria, Austria. At the eleventh hour he changed this to Transylvania after reading *Transylvanian Superstitions* (1885) by Emily de Laszowska Gerard. "The whole species of demons, pixies, witches and hobgoblins, driven by the wand of science from the rest of Europe, had taken refuge within this mountain rampart," he would have read.

Another influential work was the *Account of the Principalities of Wallachia and Moldavia* (1820), a memoir by William Wilkinson, the Consul of Bucharest. It is here that Stoker probably first encountered the name "Dracula", the inspiration for his infamous creation.

The real Dracula, Vlad Tepes (1431–76) – or Vlad the Impaler – was a violent warlord

Transylvania = "land beyond the forest"

Native Transylvanian vampire species:

- *Priculics*
- *Nosferatu*
- *Muroni*
- *Varcolaci*
- *Zmeu*
- *Strigoii or "dead vampire" (most common)*
- *Moroii, or "live vampire"*

with a reputation for torture and sadism. He killed many thousands of his enemies – and a significant number of his fellow countrymen – by impaling their bodies through the anus on wooden stakes; countless others were forced into slavery. Near the Transylvanian border, just to the north of Curtea-de-Arges, is Castle Dracula, the stronghold built by slaves under the rule of Tepes, thousands of whom are purported to have died during its construction. The castle stands to this day, and makes an excellent starting point for vampire slayers and watchers alike.

FIGURE 35

VLAD TEPES, PRINCE OF WALLACHIA, DINES AL FRESCO WHILE HIS ENEMIES ARE DISMEMBERED OR SLOWLY IMPALED ON GIANT SPIKES. ALTHOUGH A BLOODTHIRSTY WARRIOR, HE IS NEVERTHELESS A NATIONAL HERO IN HIS NATIVE ROMANIA.

The mountain-top Csejthe Castle, which overlooks the village of Csejthe in Transylvania, has also seen much bloodshed. It was home to Erzsébet Bathory (*see page 19*), the evil noblewoman who drank and bathed in the blood of her virgin servants. It is here at Csejthe Castle that she spent the last four years of her life bricked up alive in the walls. Her ghost is said to haunt the castle to this day.

† Whitby

THE ENGLISH SEASIDE TOWN of Whitby should have strong associations in the mind of the vampire watcher. This ancient fishing port, situated between the North York Moors and the North Sea at the mouth of the River Esk, is where Bram Stoker's Count Dracula arrived in England aboard the Russian schooner *Demeter*. The ship was wrecked near Tate Hill sands, with the dead captain lashed to the wheel and the crew missing. The only survivor was a large black dog that leaped from the wrecked boat and was seen running up the 199 steps of Whitby Abbey.

Stoker visited Whitby in 1890, and this short holiday was a major inspiration for the book. Many local sights feature in the novel – the lawyer who arranged the journey of Dracula to Whitby from Transylvania lived at 7 The Crescent, and the address is clearly marked. Stoker spent time observing the town from the West Cliff, from where you can clearly see the graveyard of St Mary's Church where Dracula seduced Lucy.

Back in the narrow streets and alleys of Whitby you can follow in the footsteps of Stoker. It is an atmospheric, sometimes eerie town and easy to see why it so inspired the author. Keep an eye open for other vampire

A true story! The Russian schooner Demitrius washed ashore in 1885, 10 years before Stoker paid a visit here

The Bram Stoker Memorial Seat on the southern end of the cliff is an excellent place to soak up the views that inspired the author

watchers – use the locations mentioned in the book as a guide to where you could expect to find your fellow observers.

Long before the publication of *Dracula*, Whitby already had a name as one of the most haunted or cursed areas of the British Isles, and it is likely that this paranormal reputation influenced the writer. The otherworldly black dog that fled the *Demeter*, for example, was often seen running across the moors long before Stoker incorporated it into his story.

Whitby Abbey is a good place to look for supernatural activity, as there have been many ghost sightings in and around the ruins. Its founder, St Hilda, died in AD 680 but her ghostly shrouded figure is sometimes seen in the window. The ghost of Constance de Beverley is also said to haunt the Abbey. A nun, she paid the ultimate price for an illicit dalliance with a handsome young knight: she was walled up in a dungeon, where she died a protracted and noisy death.

Look out for:
- *Vampire museums*
- *Commemorative plaques*
- *Guided tours*
- *The "Dracula Experience" (9 Marine Parade)*

Must come back for the Whitby Gothic Weekend (April and October) – could be an excellent opportunity to meet with like-minded people

APPENDIX II †

Further Reading

Walter Map, *De Nugis Curialium* ("On the Courtier's Trifles"), London, c.1100s

William of Newburgh, *Historia Rerum Anglicarum* ("History of English Affairs"), 1198

Johann Sprenger and Heinrich Kraemer, *Malleus Maleficarum* ("Witch Hammer"), Cologne, c.1485

Ludvig Lavater, *De Spectris, Lemuribus, et magnis atque insolitis Fragoribus, Variisque Praesagitionibus, quae Plerunque Obitum Hominum, Magnas Clades, Mutationesque Imperiorum Praecedunt Liber Unis* ("Of Ghosts and Spirits Walking by Night, and of Strange Noises, Cracks, and Sundry Forewarnings, which Commonly Happen Before the Death of Men, Great Slaughters, Alterations of Kingdoms"), Geneva, 1575

Henry More, *An Antidote to Atheism: or An Appeal to the Natural Faculties of the Mind of Men*, Cambridge, 1600s

Henri Boguet, *Discours des Sorciers* ("Examen of Sorcerers"), Lyons, 1603

Father Leo Allatius, *De Quorundum Graecorum Opinationibus*, Cologne, 1645

Father François Richard, *Relation du ce qui s'est passé à Sant-Erini Isle de'Archipelago* ("Relating What Occurred on the Island of Santorini in the Archipelago"), Paris, 1657

Philip Rohr, *Dissertatio Historica-Philosophica de Masticatione Mortuorum* ("Historical and Philosophical Dissertation on the Chewing Dead"), Leipzig, 1679

Charles Ferdinand de Schertz, *Magia Posthuma* ("Posthumous Magic"), Olmütz, 1706

Joseph Pitton de Tournefort, *Relations d'un Voyage du Levant* ("Account of a Voyage in the Levant"), Paris, 1717

Michael Ranftius, *De Masticatione Mortuorum in Tumulis* ("On the Masticating Dead in their Tombs"), Leipzig, 1728

Johann Flückinger, *Visum et Repurtum* ("Seen and Reported"), Austria, 1732

Christopher Rohl and Johann Hertel, *Dissertatio de Hominibus post Mortem Sanguisugis* ("Dissertation of the Bloodsucking Dead"), Leipzig, 1732

Johann Heinrich Zopfius and Charles Francis von Dalen, *Dissertatio de Vampyris* ("Dissertation on the Vampire"), Halle, 1733

Michael Ranftius, *Tractatus von dem Kauen und Schmatzen der Todten in Grabern* ("Treatise on the Chewing and Eating Dead in their Graves"), Leipzig, 1734

John Christian Harenberg, *Von Vampyren* ("On Vampires"), Wolfenbüttel, 1739

John Christian Harenberg, *Philosophicae et Christianae Cogitationes de Vampiris* ("Philosophical and Christian Thoughts on Vampires"), Wolfenbüttel, 1739

Giuseppe Davanzati, *Dissertazione sopra I Vampiri* ("Dissertation on the Vampires"), Naples, 1744

Dom Augustin Calmet, *Dissertation sur les Apparitions des Anges, des Démons, et des Esprits; et sur les Revenans et Vampires de Hongrie, de Bohême, de Moravie, et de Silésie* ("Dissertation on the Appearance of Angels, Demons and Spirits; and on the Revenants and Vampires of Hungary, of Bohemia, of Moravia, and of Silesia"), Paris, 1746

Herbert Mayo, *On the Truths Contained in Popular Superstitions*, London, 1851

Adolphe d'Assier, *Essai sur l'Humanité Posthume et le Spiritisme* ("Essay on Posthumous Humanity and Spiritism"), Paris, 1883

Franz Hartmann, *Premature Burial*, Austria, 1896

A. Osbourne Eaves, *Modern Vampirism: Its Dangers and How to Avoid Them*, Harrogate, 1904

More recent vampire references:

- Dudley Wright – "Vampires & Vampirism" William Rider & Son, London, 1914

- G. Willoughby-Meade – "Chinese Ghouls and Goblins" Constable, London, 1928

- Montague Summers – "The Vampire: Its Kith & Kin" Kegan Paul, French, Trubner & Co., London, 1928

- Montague Summers – "The Vampire in Europe" Kegan Paul, French, Trubner & Co., London, 1929

- Jan Perkowski – "Vampire of the Slavs" Slavica Publishers, Columbus, OH, 1976

- Christopher Frayling – "Vampyres: Lord Byron to Count Dracula" Faber & Faber, London, 1991

- Matthew Bunson – "Vampire: The Encyclopaedia" Crown Publishers, NY, 1993

✝

Notes

<u>Vampire societies</u>

Vampire Research Institute
Liriel McMahon
PO Box 21067
Seattle
WA 98111-3067
USA

Australian Vampyre
Information Association
PO Box 123
Mt. Gravitt Plaza
Queensland 4122
Australia

The British Vampyre
Society
38 Westcroft
Chippenham
Wiltshire
SN14 0LY
England

British Dracula Society
PO Box 30848
London
W12 0JY
England

<u>Web links</u>

www.shroudeater.com –
impressive, scholarly
reference site on European
vampire history
✳ reliable ✦ enjoyable

www.netvampyric.8m.com/
– very useful vamp portal
– lots of links ✦ discussions

www.sanguinarius.org –
support network with
health tips ✦ advice for
vampire lifestylers. Seeking
international acceptance
and tolerance to blood
drinkers.

www.pathwaystodarkness.com
– online resource & meeting
place for "real" vampires

http://vampire.the-institute
.net/vampyres/ – mailing
lists & chats; share tips
with other hunters

www.vampirelibrary.com –
well-organized & fairly
exhaustive list of books of
interest to vampire fanatics
(fiction & non-fiction)

www.digamma.com/cav
/antivampire/ – the Anti-
Vampire Centre – dedicated
to the "liberation of the
individual from vampirism"

Magazines

"Bite Me"
(www.bitememagazine.co.uk)
– news, features, reviews,
what's on
& for vampire fans

"Journal of Dracula Studies"
– magazine of the Canadian
chapter of the Transylvanian
Society of Dracula

"Black Swan"
(www.geocities.com/slarese
/index.html) – magazine
for "black swans": the
family, friends (and blood
donors) of vampires!

Index

ℐcknowledgements

AUTHOR'S ACKNOWLEDGEMENTS
My parents Sylvia and Doug; Pusan Wong;
Darren Handy; Udo; Kat Aalam (dob 1584);
Scott Christie; Helen Kelly; the Society
for Psychical Research; Angelo Plantamura;
Stacey Teale for her bottomless Buffy
knowledge; Chris Daunt for his wonderful
woodcuts; Paul Oakley for his evocative
designs; Tessa, Elaine and Ian from
Eddison Sadd; Mike Flynn for his rather
scary martial arts advice; and finally Ben
Way for all his help, advice and tireless
eyeballs.

PICTURE CREDITS
AKG London: 9, 33, 51, 100, 151; Archives
Charmet/Bridgeman Art Library: 29;
Brazzle Atkins: 76, 79, 144; Bibliothèque
Nationale, Paris: 93; Cairo, National
Museum/AKG London: 11; Corbis: 36;

Mary Evans Picture Library: 84, 117;
Fortean Picture Library: 19; Peter Jordan/
Fortean Picture Library: 64; Angelo
Plantamura: 71, 80, 103, 110, 115, 118,
121, 123, 124, 126, 135, 146.

EDDISON • SADD EDITIONS
Editorial Director Ian Jackson
Managing Editor Tessa Monina
Project Editor Terry Burrows
Proofreader Nikky Twyman
Indexer Dorothy Frame

Art Director Elaine Partington
Project Designer Paul Oakley
Picture Researcher Diana Morris
Props Deborah Thompson

Production Karyn Claridge and
Charles James